HOW TO PLAN
for College

Advisor's Guide to Acquiring New Clients and Profitable Assets

Raymond D. Loewe, MBA, CLU, ChFC
KC Dempster, ChFC

This publication is designed to provide accurate and authoritative information in regard to the subject matter covered. It is sold with the understanding that the publisher is not engaged in rendering legal, accounting or other professional service. If legal advice or other expert assistance is required, the services of a competent professional should be sought. – **From a Declaration of Principles jointly adopted by a Committee of the American Bar Association and a Committee of Publishers and Associations.**

Circular 230 Notice – The content in this publication is not intended or written to be used, and it cannot be used, for the purposes of avoiding U.S. tax penalties.

ISBN: 978-0-87218-926-3
Library of Congress Control Number: 2007931419

Printed in U. S. A.

ABOUT COLLEGE MONEY

College Money of Marlton, New Jersey is nationally recognized as a premier college financial planning firm. Founded in 1978 by Raymond D. Loewe, it has been in the business of helping parents pay for college without ruining their retirement dreams. The College Money System™ combines unique tools and strategies designed to motivate clients to take action to accomplish their goals for college and retirement.

As college costs continued to increase faster than inflation, College Money developed the Family Scholarship Plan™ to incorporate grandparents and other relatives into the college planning process.

College Money's program, "Put an Expert on Your Team," helps financial advisors deliver first class college financial planning services to their clients.

Raymond D. Loewe is recognized as a college financial planning authority on both a national and local level as evidenced by appearances on Good Morning America, CNNfn and CNBC. Further, he is frequently quoted in national and local newspapers and magazines, including the *Wall Street Journal* and *Money* magazine. Professional organizations often feature Mr. Loewe as a speaker, the most recent presentations being the Maryland Bar Association, the Annual Forum of The Society of Financial Service Professionals, and local Estate Planning Council and Financial Planning Association (FPA) groups.

Mr. Loewe has authored several books, including *A Professional's Guide to College Planning*, (published by The National Underwriting Company) as well as "New Strategies for College Funding: an Advisor's Guide" (published by John Wiley and Sons, Inc.). In recent years, Mr. Loewe has spoken on behalf of several 529 vendors to get their message in front of financial advisors while showing the advisors how to make college an effective part of their own practices.

Mr. Loewe holds an MBA from the Wharton School, University of Pennsylvania, and is a Chartered Life Underwriter (CLU) and a Chartered Financial Consultant (ChFC). As a partner with the firm, he is a Registered Principal and a Registered Financial Advisor with United Planners Financial Services of America.

KC Dempster has participated in the college planning industry for over 19 years. She has taught seminars and counseled parents on how to plan and pay for college and actually earned her bachelors degree while attending college with her children, all made possible by what she learned at College Money.

Ms. Dempster is responsible for driving College Money's "Put an Expert on Your Team" program. As a consultant to other professional advisors, she provides college financial planning expertise for their clients.

Ms. Dempster is frequently quoted in magazines and newspapers such as *The Wall Street Journal* and *Newsweek* and appeared on CN8, a regional cable provider. She has co-authored articles in industry publications and co-authored the book, *New Strategies for College Planning: an Advisor's Guide*, published by John Wiley and Sons, Inc. She holds a BS in Business Administration from Widener University, Chester, PA and is a Chartered Financial Consultant (ChFC).

TABLE OF CONTENTS

PREFACE

College costs are high and only getting higher. According to the Department of Education, there were 2,630,000 freshmen entering college in 2004. At an average 4-year cost of $100,000 per student, collectively their parents would have total 4-year college bills of $260 billion. Yes, that's *billion*! Going forward, the numbers will continue to soar. The U.S. Department of Education estimates freshman enrollment will grow to 3,800,000 in 2016, and we expect college costs to continue increasing at a rate faster than the consumer price index (CPI). Our projections show total 4-year college costs at a state university for an in-state resident student will approximate $146,000. The simple math shows parents and students could be facing a collective college bill of more than $553 billion.

This represents an enormous target market that continues to grow at approximately twice the rate of inflation. It is always surprising to us that many financial advisors either ignore this market or pay only token attention to it because we believe it can make a great target market for a financial advisory practice. And it is a market that continually renews itself. As long as parents keep having children, college will be a hot button. Therefore, the college planning market is worth learning more about as a financial advisor.

We recognized that there are five different perspectives that financial advisors can adopt toward the college planning market:

1. Some advisors choose to *ignore college financial planning* completely. Most of these advisors see a small ticket sale of college planning. They do not consider it worth their time. These advisors risk losing not only their clients' college planning business, but also the lucrative retirement sales that can follow because they are not paying attention to their clients' needs.

2. A second group of advisors are willing to *take a college planning request*, but then they don't do their homework because it takes too much time and effort for the quick, small, initial sale that results. Unfortunately, college planning can be complex. By failing to do the homework, advisors can cause more harm than good (i.e., by choosing an inappropriate product, or ignoring the implications of potential financial aid availability).

3.	Wiser financial advisors educate themselves enough to open a case and *find an expert* to take care of their client's college financial needs. Often these advisors are comfortable with their current specific area of expertise and don't want to try to be all things to all clients. They recognize that often they can bring more value to their clients by recognizing when to bring in an outside professional to help.

4.	There are also financial advisors who want to be "the expert" who helps their clients. They will expend the time and energy to learn what they need to know and will continue to educate themselves to stay up-to-date every year on all the changes that happen in the field of college financial planning.

5.	Finally, there are advisors who not only become experts, but they also realize that college financial planning can be a great *niche market* just as it has been for us.

We prepared this book primarily for advisors in Groups 3, 4, and 5. Whether you want to create a niche college planning market, or develop a strong college planning knowledge base, this book is for you. But you don't have to be a college planning expert to function effectively in this market. You can also buy outside expertise, and this book can help you develop the knowledge base to work with an expert.

Ray Loewe and KC Dempster

INTRODUCTION

We first realized that college planning would be an important part of our business in the mid-1970's. One of our clients came in and said, "Ray, I can't go ahead with this investment plan that you set up for me." Ray responded, "Okay doctor, what's the problem?" to which the doctor responded:

> "I received some good news and some bad news today. The good news is that my twin sons just got accepted to medical school. The not so good news is that I'm going to have four kids in medical school next year because the twins are joining my older son and daughter who are already in medical school. The bad news is that I just got a bill for over $80,000 for tuition for these four children and I need to scramble for the money."

This incident was the first clue that college was going to have a major impact on all of our clients; especially the wealthier ones that we thought would simply write a check to pay the college bill.

As a result we began developing a college planning process that would help our clients. Inadvertently, we also created a very valuable strategic byproduct in the form of a market niche that enhanced our financial planning practice. We found ourselves with a steady stream of potential clients in the form of upper middle-income families who cared so much about educating their children that they were willing to jeopardize their retirement.

The College Money System™ that emerged—a series of workshops, concepts, tools, and strategies—became the only way we needed to market our financial planning practice. Other than direct referrals, college planning workshops became our sole way of acquiring new clients because:

- College planning is extremely efficient. It allows us to educate prospects, all at once, in a short, structured workshop. The prospects then come into our office pre-educated and prepared to discuss a problem that's both important and urgent to them. They're ready to take action!

- As you will see, college planning allows us to filter through a group of prospects to effectively "screen-in" only those that meet our criteria to become clients.

Because many aspects of college financial planning can be complex, we often found that clients had difficulty understanding what we were explaining. Unfortunately, they didn't always let us know that they were confused; they simply didn't take action. Over time we developed a series of interactive tools that turned spreadsheets into moving graphs. This visual perspective helped our clients grasp our message very quickly and the delays in taking action virtually disappeared.

Several of the models that we use in our practice appear in this book. They include:

- The College Planning Conversation™: This model demonstrates the relationship between paying for college and its effect on retirement. It gets clients' attention!

- The Financial Aid Appraisal™: The value of the Financial Aid Appraisal™ is that it can forecast potential future financial aid. Often parents hold on to the hope that they will qualify for aid and, therefore, delay or ignore saving. Showing what percentage of college costs they can truly expect need-based financial to cover is a great reality check and motivates parents to start saving.

- The Real Grandparent College Contribution™:- Grandparents often don't appreciate how much impact a gift toward a college fund can have. This model demonstrates just how helpful grandparents' contributions actually can be.

Not only are these models used as illustrations in the book, working versions are included in the kit for your use. College Money developed the engines that drive the models and we use them in our every day financial planning practice to get results. The underlying data comes from various respected sources such as the United States Census Bureau, the United States Department of Education, and the College Board.

Readers might notice that the versions of the software in the book are slightly modified from the ones available through our website in that the book versions don't use the benchmark colleges that we use in our own projections. The book versions of the software allow the planner to input any college cost desired. Please refer to Appendix A for a discussion of why we use benchmark colleges in our own projections, as well as our methodology for determining the college costs on which we base the projections.

Most of the revenue in our practice comes from something we call the "college/retirement sale." Although college is the trigger that brings prospects to our doorstep, college and retirement are so closely related that it becomes easy to leap from the college problem to the retirement problem *if it's handled carefully*. Only about 10% to 20% of our revenue actually comes from college funding products, but the college planning process quickly leads to a discussion of retirement and ultimately to acquiring a client's retirement assets. Of the three college planning periods—*saving*, *spending* and *borrowing*, and *recovery*—it's the recovery period that creates the urgency for solving the retirement problem.

Another reason we get so excited about college funding is that the sale of college and retirement products has helped us create a substantial six-figure, ongoing income stream of trailer commissions. This led to a comfortable working environment that allowed us to hire a substantial staff and to know that there's enough income coming in through the year on a predictable basis that we can cover our overhead. Any revenue generated from new business, over and above the trailers, gives us the capital to explore new opportunities.

There's another factor that makes college an ideal vehicle for approaching clients—it's built around the *emotional* nature of college education. Most of our clients care deeply about their children. They want the best for them and are willing to make substantial sacrifices. This makes college a nonthreatening, easy to discuss event. We all know that sales are made not on logic, but on emotion. When you have an opportunity to help a prospect or client do really good things for their children it leads to a better relationship that tends to be stronger over the long haul.

I have to take a moment here to talk about my "Uncle Ray" relationship with my college planning clients. Because we have worked with so many families on their college problems, it is not uncommon to get invited to a lot of high school graduation parties. In fact there were so many that I literally had to stop going to them because I was starting to gain a lot of weight. But I made an exception in one particular case. The father was a caterer and I figured the food would really be great. When I walked into the house, there was a magnificent display of food just as I expected. All of a sudden a young lady ran up to me, wrapped her arms around me, gave me a big hug and said:

> "My mom and dad told me that I wouldn't be going to the college I'm going to if it weren't for you. Thank you Uncle Ray."

Now the results of the story are interesting because not only did we get the college planning sales from this family, but we also got the life insurance, health insurance, retirement plans, and the other savings and investment accounts. But even more important is the strength of the "Uncle Ray" relationship. I'm not viewed as just the financial advisor for this family, even though that's what I am. Instead, they treat me as a family member—the uncle who helped put the kids through college. And "Uncle Ray" gets more opportunities to make things right when they aren't working so well. It's easier to keep your client relationship and to keep investment plans on the books when you have an "Uncle Ray" relationship as opposed to simply a financial advisor relationship.

College planning also leads to multi-generational sales. Recently we had husband-and-wife dentists walk into our office. We had helped each of their parents put them through college. Now they're married and planning for college for their two children. College Money™ was a natural place for them to come. Needless to say we're not discussing only college plans, but we're also talking about retirement and helping them set up their own practice.

Another facet of multi-generational planning comes from setting up Family Scholarship Plans™, which allow us to bring grandparents into a plan set up by parents or, conversely, bring parents into a plan set up by grandparents. And when the college planning process is complete, it easy to begin a discussion about the grandparents' or the parents' personal needs. (We'll discuss these plans more in a later chapter.)

Needless to say, we tend to get excited about what college planning has done for our firm. We hope that throughout the rest of this book you will get excited about college planning as a tool to grow your business.

Chapter 1

COLLEGE PLANNING AS A MARKETING FOCUS

When it comes to saving for college, parents can be great procrastinators. On the one hand, parents know that a college savings plan is something that they need to come to grips with. Yet on the other hand, college seems so far away, and there are so many other day-to-day problems involving raising children that it's easy to put off taking action when it comes to saving for college.

Recently, a couple attended one of our workshops, came up to us afterward, and informed us that they wanted to start planning early to get a handle on college. Their son was a high school junior!

Unfortunately, the example above is more of a typical case than a rare one. As financial advisors, we can make a difference by making sure that parents understand the magnitude of the college problem and, most important, the effect that it's going to have on their ability to retire later on if they *don't* deal with it now. There are several factors/myths in particular that influence a parents' inclination to procrastinate:

1. Most parents severely underestimate the cost of college. If they really knew what college was going to cost, they would be motivated to act much sooner.

2. Many parents hope their talented children will win an academic, talent, or athletic scholarship. But these scholarships are harder to win than most parents realize and depending on them in lieu of saving can be foolhardy.

3. Some parents don't feel wealthy, so they are certain that they will qualify for financial aid. They

I remember talking to a very proud dad about his All-State football-playing son who had a guaranteed scholarship to a Big Ten College. The son injured his leg in the last high school football game of the year so seriously that he will never play football again. Unfortunately, the scholarship was withdrawn as a result of the injury. It had been tied to the son's ability to play football.

don't realize that financial aid is heavily driven by parent income, and income often rises just before college starts.

If we want parents to take action, it's important for us as advisors to address each of these factors/myths early in the planning process.

QUANTIFYING THE COLLEGE PROBLEM

The first step in solving the college problem is to determine what college *really* costs. This seems like an easy task, but in reality it's not. There are a *lot* of misconceptions about college costs. We repeatedly ask parents what they think the college they graduated from would cost today. Most have no clue. This isn't a surprising result when one thinks about it. Many of these parents didn't pay for their own college education; in most cases, their parents did. They were never aware of what college cost even back then. In addition, parents aren't focused on college costs—and understandably so. They're focused on making a living and raising their children. Usually its only when college approaches that they really begin to focus on what college really costs.

> Most parents *severely* underestimate the cost of college and this drastically affects their planning.

Another major contributing factor is that college costs are often undervalued by the media. They refer to tuition, only, or to tuition room and board. But tuition, room, and board are only *part* of the total cost of college. College costs also include books, fees, transportation, laundry money, miscellaneous personal expenses, and even networking money.

Avoid Using Specific Colleges When Planning

When creating savings projections for college, it is advisable to use average costs for a class of colleges rather than a specific college. Our experience is that colleges have different cost centers that they can control, such as, tuition and fees, and room and board. Often the administration may decide to artificially hold down the cost of tuition for a period of time. Occasionally, college costs for a specific college may rise meteorically because of a change in policy. For example, the University of Richmond's costs have increased disproportionately in recent years because of a change in the administration's strategy.

By making projections for typical college costs based on the *type* of college within a class (i.e. Ivy League college, state college for in-state residency, etc.), planners can smooth out some of the peaks and valleys and still bring the family's plan in on target.

Parents and students shouldn't underestimate the value or the cost of networking. Part of the value of college is what students learn, but an equally substantial part consists of the people they meet. We've all heard the expression, "it's not *what* you know but *who* you know" that really counts. A future entrepreneur or business person can't meet future business and professional contacts by sitting alone in their dormitory room. They need to get out and socialize. This may mean joining a fraternity or sorority, joining late night study sessions, or simply getting involved in other campus events. These activities usually cost money and, therefore, should be budgeted as part of the total cost of college.

Some add in extra costs, such as for pizza or networking, to college costs. However, such costs are not eligible for financial aid or for special treatment with respect to investments in tax favored education accounts, such as 529 plans. Also, some persons do not believe that such costs are truly part of planning for future college costs: such costs are incurred now, and will be in the future, and are simply paid in the normal course of events by the parent or the child. So it may be useful to run calculations with and without the extra costs.

Finally, it's not very easy to get a handle on college cost data. Although most colleges have a website, and somewhere on this website is a list of costs, it's often difficult to find the right web page. Some colleges list their costs under the financial aid section while others list their costs in the admissions section. Different academic programs often have different costs (e.g., engineering school costs are different than, and usually higher than, liberal arts program costs). To further complicate matters, many college websites aren't updated on a frequent basis. For example, many state colleges don't update their tuition costs until as late as September. This is generally due to late approval of a college budget by the state legislature.

Parents and advisors can't plan without having a good idea of what college costs *today* and what it will cost in the *future*. Figure 1.1 gives a summary of the components of college costs.

Some parents feel that some of the costs of college are not their responsibility (i.e., they can pass these costs on to their children). But the planning stage is not necessarily the time to decide who's going to pay what. It's simply the time to get a handle on what the total cost of college will be. Nevertheless, it is important to remember that all costs are not eligible for financial aid or for special treatment with respect to investments in tax favored education accounts, such as 529 accounts.

Figure 1.1: Components of College Costs

Tuition and fees	Fees may include graduation fees, course specific fees, health insurance fees, etc.
Room and board	There may be a variety of meal plans to choose from or the school might have one mandated meal plan.
Books and supplies	Notebooks; special clothing related to a specific course; might include a computer if the school requires one.
Personal expenses	Laundry money and supplies, toiletries, social events like football games, etc.
Transportation	Parents generally want their children to come home for holidays.
Networking	Fraternity/sorority dues, pizza out with friends, etc.

Figure 1.2 gives a summary of some typical college types and what they cost today.

Figure 1.2: Typical College Costs

Average Undergraduate Tuition, Fees, and Room and Board (R+B)		
	2004-2005*	**2007-2008****
2-Year Institution (no R+B)	$2,323	$2,919
2-Year Institution (w/ R+B)	$7,020	$8,821
4-Year Public Institution (no R+B)	$5,038	$6,331
4-Year Public Institution (w/ R+B)	$11,441	$14,376
4-Year Private Institution (w/ R+B)	$26,489	$33,285
4-Year All Institutions (w/ R+B)	$16,465	$20,689

*Source: U.S. Department of Education, National Center for Education Statistics. Public institution costs are for in-state.
**Projected at 7.91% college inflation rate.

It's bad enough that college costs are so high today. But parents of young children also have to worry about *college* inflation and the reality that college inflation has been running about twice what normal inflation (i.e., the consumer price index or CPI) has been running.

Figure 1.3 is a summary of the last 28 years of college inflation versus CPI. It is clear that college inflation is a significant factor in the college planning arena.

College inflation has been higher than CPI every year after 1980. On average it has been almost two times as high as CPI; consequently, advisors and their clients need to recognize this and factor this in when setting savings goals.

Figure 1.3: A History of College Inflation vs. CPI

Year	College Inflation	CPI	Difference
Average	**8.08%**	**4.15%**	**3.93%**
2006	7.06%	3.82%	3.24%
2005	7.33%	3.64%	3.69%
2004	8.43%	2.65%	5.78%
2003	9.53%	2.16%	7.37%
2002	7.10%	1.80%	5.30%
2001	5.64%	2.72%	2.92%
2000	4.26%	3.41%	0.85%
1999	3.94%	2.26%	1.68%
1998	3.89%	1.62%	2.27%
1997	5.12%	2.23%	2.89%
1996	5.71%	2.88%	2.83%
1995	6.39%	2.62%	3.77%
1994	7.24%	2.90%	4.34%
1993	9.32%	2.77%	6.55%
1992	11.43%	3.15%	8.28%
1991	8.74%	3.80%	4.94%
1990	9.17%	5.62%	3.55%
1989	7.82%	4.71%	3.11%
1988	8.40%	4.02%	4.38%
1987	8.74%	4.28%	4.46%
1986	8.36%	1.57%	6.79%
1985	9.33%	3.35%	5.98%
1984	10.29%	4.29%	6.00%
1983	10.58%	2.56%	8.02%
1982	14.01%	5.85%	8.16%
1981	12.23%	10.80%	1.43%
1980	8.19%	12.87%	-4.68%
1979	7.99%	11.82%	-3.83%

Source - CPI Data: U.S. Department Of, Bureau of Labor Statistics, Consumer Price Index, All Urban Consumers - (CPI-U), U.S. city average All items, 1982-84=100, September 1 to August 31
Source - College Inflation CPI-U, College Tuition and Fees

Parents keep telling us that college inflation can't continue at this pace. However, it appears not only that it can, but that it will. There are primarily two reasons why college inflation is running rampant:

1.   College is a labor-intensive industry. Quality professors demand quality salaries. And this is going to continue to drive college inflation. It can be argued that it might be possible to cut costs by using Internet courses, and the Internet can be an effective way of transmitting educational material. But the Internet doesn't foster effective networking.

2.   Probably the biggest factor causing college costs to soar is supply and demand. Last year, Ray's alma mater, The University of Pennsylvania, had approximately 18,000 applicants for 2,000 spots in the freshman class and the right to pay almost $50,000 in total costs. With this type of demand, there is no reason for this school to lower costs. It seems as though they have an unlimited supply of applicants. A student who declines a place in the freshman class because of cost will quickly be replaced by a student with parents who are willing and able to write the check. Furthermore, high costs seem to carry a prestige factor. The higher the cost, the more the school is perceived to be "better" than the others; consequently, parents want to have their children go there.

Another worrisome factor is that costs for state colleges—the so-called "cheap" college alternative—seem to be rising faster than private school costs. Why? The reason is that in this time of increasing taxes and costs, the public doesn't seem to be willing to continue to support public colleges. Because of this, a lot of the costs formerly subsidized by the government are being transferred to the student in the form of tuition, fee, and room and board cost increases. What all this means is that future college costs are going to continue to rise—probably at an alarming rate.

Just how big could this college problem become? The table on page 7 shows typical total college costs 10 years into the future.

THE COLLEGE PLANNING CONVERSATION™

In order to move the college problem towards a solution, financial advisors should have a College Planning Conversation™ with their clients. The purpose of the College Planning Conversation is to get clients to focus on the college problem. Clients need to understand that failing to plan for college can have a dramatic effect on their ability to retire. As part of that process, they should understand that there are three distinct college planning periods:

Average Undergraduate Tuition, Fees, and Room and Board In 10 Years

| | Year | 2-Year Institutions | | 4-Year Institutions | | | |
		no R+B	w/ R+B	Public*	Public	Private	All
Freshman	2016	$5,791	$17,502	$12,560	$28,524	$66,040	$41,049
Sophomore	2017	$6,250	$18,886	$13,554	$30,780	$71,264	$44,296
Junior	2018			$14,626	$33,214	$76,901	$47,800
Senior	2019			$15,783	$35,842	$82,983	$51,581
Total		$12,041	$36,388	$56,523	$128,360	$297,187	$184,725

Costs are projected at a 7.91% college inflation rate from college costs obtained from the U.S. Department of Education, National Center for Education Statistics.
Public institution costs are for in-state.

*No room and board (R+B) for this column

1. the *savings period*, which begins today and lasts through the first day of college;

2. the *spending/borrowing period*, which begins the day college starts and ends the day college stops; and

3. the *recovery period*, which begins the day college ends and lasts through the day the clients want the college problem to go away—usually no later than the beginning of retirement.

Clients must also understand that procrastination can mean losing the use of one of these three college planning periods. If a client ignores saving money for college during the savings period, he doesn't get another savings period. It's gone! His only recourse is to use the next period—the spending and borrowing period—which means taking more money out of current income during the college years, or borrowing. Paying for college is very much a "pay me a *little* more *now*, or pay me a *lot* more *later* on. The choice is yours." The increasing pressure on the family can ultimately result in a retirement problem down the road. The easiest way to demonstrate this is to review a College Planning Conversation with a typical client.

We began the process by asking John and Mary Sample (age 40 and 38), typical college planning parents, to tell us a little bit about their children and their college desires for them. John began by telling us that he and Mary have two children. Brittany should start college in 2016 and Connor should follow two years later in 2018. When we asked the Samples what kind of college they would like to plan for, they gave us a typical answer: "We're not sure. We would like our children to go to whatever school is appropriate for them."

Both John and Mary, however, attended state colleges as in-state students. After a brief discussion, they decided to plan for each of their children based on state college costs as in-state students ($19,000 for 2006-2007, in this case, at Rutgers in New Jersey), and to make adjustments to their plan as they get closer to the start of college.

Figure 1.4 contains a bar graph showing how much the Samples will pay each year for college. When Brittany starts college, the Samples will need to have almost $37,000 ready to go. Note from the bar graph that two spikes occur when two children are in college at the same time. In those years, the Samples need to be prepared to spend approximately $87,000 and $94,000, respectively. Keep in mind that these are the Samples' goals and this is their plan. The advisor is not determining the college bill, the Samples are. Overall, they are going to spend almost $366,000 to pay for two children to attend four years, each, as in-state students at a state university.

Next, we asked the Samples to tell us their plan for funding these college goals. They indicated that:

- They want to start their plan early in 2007.

- They hope to save $400 every month ($4,800 annually) throughout the savings/investment period (i.e., beginning now and continuing through the beginning of college).

- They feel that during the spending/borrowing period (beginning the first year of college and ending the last year of college), they could come up with $12,000 each year towards college expenses.

- The Samples plan to retire in 2032, and they want to have all college debts paid before they enter retirement.

- The Samples are moderately conservative investors. They feel a 7.5% earnings rate on their savings is appropriate.

- Since the Samples may need to borrow money, we suggested that they use a 9% borrowing rate. When forecasting interest rates well into the future, the Samples wanted to be conservative. Nine percent is the guaranteed cap on the federal PLUS loan, which allows most parents to borrow all the needed funds for college.

Figure 1.4

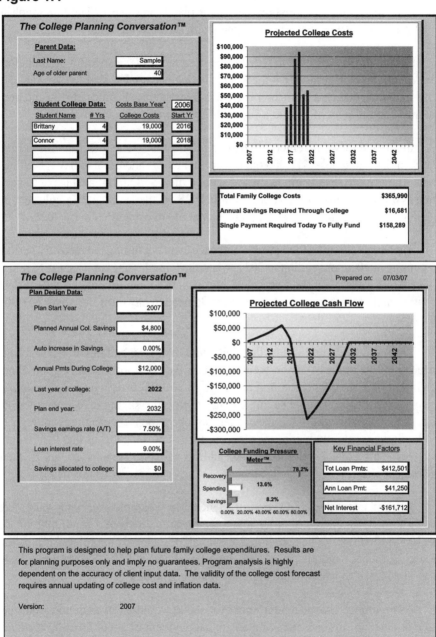

The College Planning Conversation™

Parent Data:

Last Name: Sample
Age of older parent: 40

Student College Data:

Student Name	# Yrs	College Costs	Start Yr
Brittany	4	19,000	2016
Connor	4	19,000	2018

Costs Base Year*: 2006

Projected College Costs

Total Family College Costs	$365,990
Annual Savings Required Through College	$16,681
Single Payment Required Today To Fully Fund	$158,289

The College Planning Conversation™   Prepared on: 07/03/07

Plan Design Data:

Plan Start Year	2007
Planned Annual Col. Savings	$4,800
Auto increase in Savings	0.00%
Annual Pmts During College	$12,000
Last year of college:	2022
Plan end year:	2032
Savings earnings rate (A/T)	7.50%
Loan interest rate	9.00%
Savings allocated to college:	$0

Projected College Cash Flow

College Funding Pressure Meter™

Recovery 78.2%
Spending 13.6%
Savings 8.2%
0.00% 20.00% 40.00% 60.00% 80.00%

Key Financial Factors

Tot Loan Pmts:	$412,501
Ann Loan Pmt:	$41,250
Net Interest	-$161,712

This program is designed to help plan future family college expenditures. Results are for planning purposes only and imply no guarantees. Program analysis is highly dependent on the accuracy of client input data. The validity of the college cost forecast requires annual updating of college cost and inflation data.

Version: 2007

*2006 – 2007

Now that the Samples have stated their college goals and indicated their plan for achieving them, let's see how well their plan would work. The line graph in Figure 1.5 shows what is going to happen with the Samples' plan.

During the savings period—that is, beginning in 2007 and ending right before Brittany begins college in 2016—the Samples would accumulate slightly over $58,000. This figure would come from their current college savings balance of zero and their savings commitment of $4,800 a year at a 7.5% compounded growth rate.

In 2016, they would enter the spending/borrowing period. During this period, the Samples would take $12,000 out of current income and use it to pay for college bills. They would then begin to draw down on their $58,000 of savings until such time as it was depleted. This would occur in 2018. At that point, the Samples would begin borrowing and would accumulate a debt of almost $265,000 by 2021.

The Samples would then need to amortize this debt during the recovery period, beginning in 2022 and ending in 2031, when the Samples should be ready to retire. Since this is a relatively short period of time, the cost of amortizing the college debt is rather high. In this case, the Samples would need to pay out a little over $41,000 per year to get out of debt.

We asked the Samples how they felt about their plan and immediately recognized from the expressions on their faces that they did not feel very good about it. *In fact, the Samples' plan had managed to turn their college problem into a retirement problem.* By not saving enough during the saving/investment period, they had simply moved the bulk of their college expenses into the recovery period with very little time until the start of retirement. This meant that they would be paying off college bills instead of adding valuable savings dollars to their retirement plans.

After an uncomfortable period of silence, Mary Sample sheepishly said, "We weren't going to tell you about this, but we recently received a small inheritance of about $100,000. We've committed about half of it already to projects around the house. But what would happen if we put a lump sum of $50,000 into our college plan in addition to what we are currently planning on doing."

As Figure 1.6 shows, a lump sum of $50,000 would make a significant difference in the plan. Instead of having an annual payment of about $41,000 to amortize debt during the recovery period, the Samples would be able to reduce this to approximately $19,000, less than one-half the amount required under the original plan. All of a sudden their plan becomes possible!

Figure 1.5

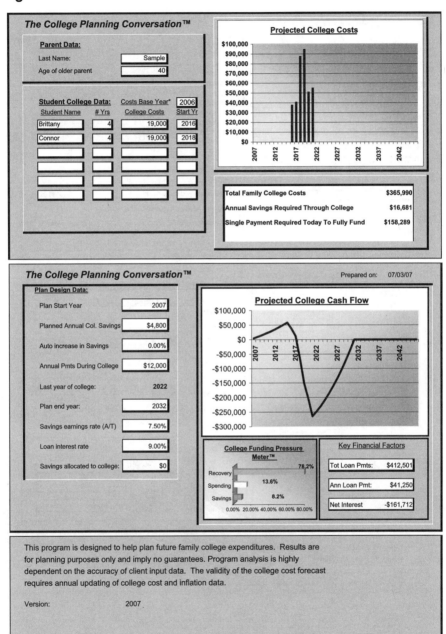

The College Planning Conversation™

Parent Data:

Last Name: Sample
Age of older parent 40

Student College Data: Costs Base Year* 2006

Student Name	# Yrs	College Costs	Start Yr
Brittany	4	19,000	2016
Connor	4	19,000	2018

Projected College Costs

Total Family College Costs	$365,990
Annual Savings Required Through College	$16,681
Single Payment Required Today To Fully Fund	$158,289

The College Planning Conversation™ Prepared on: 07/03/07

Plan Design Data:

Plan Start Year	2007
Planned Annual Col. Savings	$4,800
Auto increase in Savings	0.00%
Annual Pmts During College	$12,000
Last year of college:	2022
Plan end year:	2032
Savings earnings rate (A/T)	7.50%
Loan interest rate	9.00%
Savings allocated to college:	$0

Projected College Cash Flow

College Funding Pressure Meter™

Recovery 78.2%
Spending 13.6%
Savings 8.2%

0.00% 20.00% 40.00% 60.00% 80.00%

Key Financial Factors

Tot Loan Pmts:	$412,501
Ann Loan Pmt:	$41,250
Net Interest	-$161,712

This program is designed to help plan future family college expenditures. Results are for planning purposes only and imply no guarantees. Program analysis is highly dependent on the accuracy of client input data. The validity of the college cost forecast requires annual updating of college cost and inflation data.

Version: 2007

*2006 – 2007

Figure 1.6

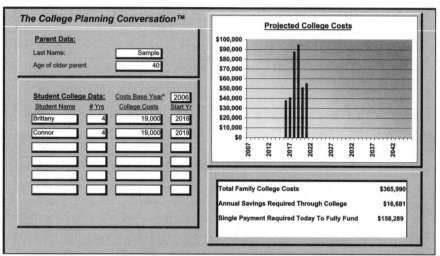

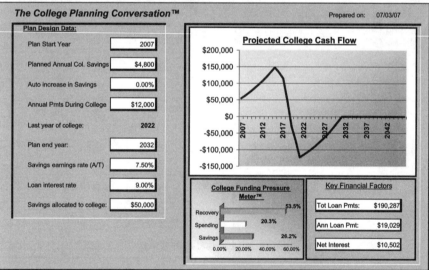

This program is designed to help plan future family college expenditures. Results are for planning purposes only and imply no guarantees. Program analysis is highly dependent on the accuracy of client input data. The validity of the college cost forecast requires annual updating of college cost and inflation data.

Version: 2007

*2006 – 2007

Lump sums deposited early in a college savings plan can make a major difference due to compound interest. Unfortunately, most parents don't have lump sums to invest in their college savings plans. Often, however, grandparents do. More on how grandparents can help will follow in Chapter 5.

The visualization of the recovery period can be a major motivating factor for parents to take action. Suddenly, college is not just a college problem—it's a problem that impacts the parents' ability to retire. We saw the effect that the visual depiction of the recovery period had on Mary Sample. Suddenly, she was motivated to tell us about discretionary funds she had not previously disclosed, and was willing to use those funds to take action.

We've had other indications that the recovery period can be a strong motivating factor to do more to save for college. We were recently engaged to do a study by the human resources department of a major credit card company. While doing college planning workshops for them, we had noticed that although rank-and-file employees filled up the workshop, they were not getting participation from their executives. In addition this company had a company-sponsored 529 college savings plan, and they were wondering why their executives were not participating in the 529 plan either. We were asked to conduct the College Planning Conversation™ with a dozen company executives to see how they would react.

The executives had incomes ranging from $150,000 annually at the low end to $500,000 at the high end. Each had children below the high school level. When shown the results of their initial college plan through The College Planning Conversation, every one of the executives looked at the recovery period with dismay. In every instance, they were surprised by the inadequacy of their college savings plans. One even commented:

> "That's not a recovery period, that's a 'well of terror.' You have to tell me what to do to make this go away. I'm working like a dog for this company so that when my children are finished with college I'll have the ability to bail out and go play golf. I can't do that with this amount of college debt in the picture."

Once they understood the impact that college was going to have on their ability to retire each executive made significant contributions to the company 529 plan to help get rid of "the well of terror." These ranged from a minimum commitment of $500 a month to a maximum commitment of a $250,000 lump sum contribution plus the commitment of the executive's deferred bonus of approximately $100,000 a year for the next five years.

> Getting parents to understand and visualize the college/retirement link is the key to motivating parents to take significant college planning action.

Chapter 2

FINDING YOUR COLLEGE PLANNING PROSPECTS

The college savings market is really an upper middle income market. Although rich families and poor families alike want to send their children to college, lower-income families generally won't be in a position to make much of a difference in saving for college. Instead, they need to focus on their own retirement and prepare to capitalize on financial aid eligibility, if possible.

On the other hand, upper middle income families will probably write checks to the colleges themselves. They really need financial advising and guidance because they must prepare for college and retirement *at the same time*. In all likelihood these families won't get much help from the financial aid system. The savings period will be critical for these folks. Fortunately, most college funding products are also wealth management products, ones that tend to offer tax incentives that help higher income families.

As a financial advisor, it is possible to help both lower and higher income families. But we recommend focusing most of your energy on the higher income group, which should be your target market. One way to accomplish this is to use workshops to educate parents. A good workshop gives families a comprehensive blueprint for attacking the college problem. A good workshop also provides information. Many financial advisors fear that if they don't hold back information in a workshop, attendees won't need to come in to see them. But if the workshop is comprehensive: it should provide lower income families and do it yourselfers with enough information to do it themselves, while motivating the upper income individuals to seek more assistance. We've found that this is the preferred result. Lower income families and do-it-yourselfers are not the advisor's most desirable clients. By helping them to do-it-themselves, the advisor can filter them out of the prospecting base in a very positive way so that they leave the workshop happy. Meanwhile, the higher income, non do-it-yourselfers that are left will come in to see the advisor. This group makes up the best potential client group for the advisor.

The workshop content should help attendees develop priorities with respect to the college/retirement problem. These priorities are to:

1.   maximize retirement savings;

2.   maximize financial aid eligibility; and

3.   channel discretionary cash into appropriate college funding vehicles.

Before starting a college savings plan, parents need to be saving substantial amounts for their own retirement. There are unsecured loans available for college, but no one would be willing to make an unsecured loan for retirement. There is financial aid available for college, but no financial aid for retirement. At the very least, parents should be funding their 401(k) plans up to the employer match (and this still might not be enough) before they consider funding a college plan.

Retirement savings usually do not affect financial aid negatively. Lower income families are typically eligible for financial aid. As family income rises, financial aid eligibility falls. So *income* is the dominant negative factor in receiving financial aid, although improperly structured *assets* can also have a major negative effect. A simple financial aid test can tell a parent quickly whether or not his student will get financial aid assistance and provide an indication of how much aid the student might receive (see the Financial Aid Test™ and the Financial Aid Appraisal™ in Chapter 8).

Only when retirement savings are under control and financial aid resources are fully explored should an advisor move on to more comprehensive college planning. Three good target markets for college savings plans are:

1.   *Business executives earning $150,000 and more.* People in this income range usually won't qualify for much financial aid. In addition, workplace retirement plans and an employer match to a 401(k) account means that executives will generally have retirement at least somewhat in hand. Many executives, however, want to retire early so there will be a shorter recovery period. This means that there will be more pressure to fund college in order to reduce the need for college loans that could inhibit the executive's ability to retire. Lastly, there is usually discretionary income available for college funding, but the advisor may need to change the executive's thinking about deferred bonuses or stock option plans in order to find it.

2.   *Doctors.* In addition to having high incomes and little-to-no financial aid eligibility, these professionals know the value of education and they tend to be predisposed to investing in college funding plans.

3.   *Grandparents* often have cash and a desire to give something special to their grandchildren.

Figure 2.1 Prioritize Saving for College, Financial Aid, and Saving for Retirement When Prospecting for Clients

Family Income	Under $75,000	Between $75,000 and $150,000	Over $150,000
Retirement Savings	Important	Important	Important
Financial Aid	Higher	Lower	Usually not Available
Eligibility Discretionary Income Available for College Funding	Usually not available	Maybe available	Usually available

THE FAMILY SCHOLARSHIP PLAN™

One of the things that we learned in dealing with clients is never to jump to a financial product as a solution too quickly. This is particularly important when dealing with college planning issues because many times clients have been misinformed about key products that we would like to use. For example, not too long ago we were discussing 529 plans with one of our clients. He immediately commented:

"I just read about those in the Wall Street Journal. Those are those things with the high fees. I don't want one of them."

A statement like that in the early discussion of college savings plan design can be troublesome. If the client is adamant in his position, he could end up with a less than optimal plan. Our solution to this dilemma was to create the Family Scholarship Plan. The Family Scholarship Plan is useful for two reasons. First, it gets the client to focus on his objectives and benefits as opposed to a financial product. Second, it gives us an opportunity to bring the family into the college planning solution.

It's important to realize that a Family Scholarship Plan is not a product, it's a strategy. There are two parts to the Family Scholarship Plan, which can be viewed in Figure 2.2. First, there's a financial toolbox that lists the financial products we might decide to use as part of a college planning solution. I explain to the client that this is *my* toolbox, not his. What I need the client to focus on are the benefits he might like to find in his college plan. The potential benefits are also listed in

Figure 2.2. Although this list is not all-inclusive, we have found that these are the primary benefits/goals that clients can usually derive from a well-constructed college savings plan.

Figure 2.2

The Family Scholarship Plan™
... a strategy, not a product

Benefits

- ❏ **Tax-Free Accumulation**
- ❏ **Tax-Free Distribution**
- ❏ **Distribution Control**
- ❏ **Investment Control**
- ❏ **Estate Tax Reduction**
- ❏ **Medical Planning**
- ❏ **Creditor Protection**
- ❏ **Financial Aid Enhancement**
- ❏ **Private School Availability**
- ❏ **Special Needs**

The College Funding Toolbox

529 Plans – Savings/Prepaid

Coverdell ESA

UGMA/UTMA

Life Insurance

Other Investments

May Require Multiple Tools to Achieve Desired Benefits

When reviewing the benefits list with a client, it's important to differentiate between the benefits desired by the *owner* of the contract and those desired by the *beneficiary* of the contract. For example, when a parent is setting up a Family Scholarship Plan for his children, the benefits are usually the same for the parent and the child. But, if a grandparent is setting up a plan for a grandchild, the benefits required can be quite different. The best way to understand how to use the benefits first when building a Family Scholarship Plan is to review an example.

Different Plans for Different Grandchildren

Chuck and Ann have two children and four grandchildren. Chuck is an architect and owns his own firm. Ann is a teacher. They have a good income and are not quite ready to retire. Chuck and Ann would like to help with college costs for their grandchildren, but know they can't fully fund a college plan.

We asked Chuck to review the benefits list from the Family Scholarship Plan. Chuck commented that he would like to incorporate both *tax-free accumulation* and *tax-free distribution* into his plan. He commented that both of these benefits were important because he is in a high tax bracket. Obviously, he didn't want to pay taxes during the accumulation period or during the distribution period, if possible.

Chuck indicated that *distribution control* is also very important. He wants to put money aside for college and does not want his grandchildren to have access to this money unless they are using it to pay for education. When it comes to *investment control*, Chuck commented that although he would like to have some say over the matter that was a primary responsibility, he was willing to delegate to me as his advisor.

In reviewing the rest of the list, Chuck commented, "I really don't see anything else that jumps out at me except perhaps for *private school availability*." Chuck continued, "I sent my children to private high school. If it's possible to help my grandchildren go to private high school and if it's appropriate, I would like to take advantage of that feature."

Next, we asked Chuck a little about his son, Brian. Chuck's response was that Brian is either going to be the next multimillionaire in this country, or he's going to be totally bankrupt. When Brian got out of college, according to Chuck, instead of getting a "real job" he bought a mattress company franchise. He has since parlayed this into ownership of several mattress company franchise stores. Brian is doing extremely well. He is making a lot of money, but he is also reinvesting all of his earnings into his next store. He's highly leveraged and, therefore, at risk financially if things go wrong.

Later, we met with Brian and talked about his needs in a college savings plan. Brian commented that he was in a high tax bracket and therefore *tax-free accumulation* and *tax-free distribution* were both important. He wasn't concerned about the other things on the list except for *creditor protection*. He commented that "in the event I have a business problem, I certainly don't want the funds that grandpa sets aside for college for my children to be in jeopardy."

The Family Scholarship Plan that we recommended in the example for Chuck, Ann, and for their son Brian, used two different tools from our toolbox. First, we invested the maximum amount into a Coverdell Education Savings Account (ESA) for each child. Second, we invested the balance of Chuck and Ann's contribution into a Section 529 college savings plan. Chuck was the owner of both plans and Brian's children were the beneficiaries.

The plan seemed to meet all of Chuck's, Ann's, and Brian's needs. First, use of the ESA allowed money to be used tax-free for private high school. Any money from this account could later be rolled into a Section 529 plan savings account without penalty if not used for private high school. (Please note ESAs may be less useful after 2011 because some of the special features recently permanently extended to 529 plans were not extended to ESAs.)

The use of these two tools gave Chuck and Brian all of the tax advantages they wished to have. In addition, because Chuck is the owner of the savings plans it is highly unlikely that Brian's creditors would have any access to money in the plan should Brian have future business problems. The result was a plan that met everyone's objectives.

When it came to Chuck and Ann's plan for their daughter Julie, we encountered a series of different concerns. Julie was trained as a schoolteacher. She is married to Ed, who is also a schoolteacher. But Julie is currently a stay-at-home mom, so she is not earning income. Total family income for Julie and Ed is approximately $50,000 per year. When Julie looked at the benefits checklist for The Family Scholarship Plan, the only item she was concerned about was financial aid. Her comment was, "It's great that mom and dad are putting aside money for college; however, unless they fully fund college, it's important to me to keep my financial aid eligibility options open. I may need financial aid if I want my kids to be able to attend quality schools."

Consequently, the plan that Chuck and Ann set up for Julie's children was very different from the plan they had set up for Brian's children. This time, Chuck and Ann used an overfunded variable life insurance policy, which was overfunded in order to put the emphasis on building cash value. Chuck was the owner of the policy and Ed, the son-in-law, was the insured. The plan is that when Julie's children are ready for college, Julie will apply for financial aid. After Julie receives her financial aid package, Chuck will make withdrawals or take policy loans and give the difference between the financial aid award and the cost of college to either (1) Julie, (2) Julie and Ed, or (3) to Julie, Ed, and the children, depending upon the gift tax restrictions at the time. The gifts of money would be immediately expended to pay college bills. Because Chuck would own the policy, and because the gifts to Julie's family would be expended immediately, this plan would have little, if any, effect on Julie's kids' ability to qualify for financial aid.

One of the problems with using a variable life insurance policy to fund college expenses is that the returns on the investment will most likely be lower than the returns using an equivalent 529 plan. The reason for this is the cost of life insurance. In this case, however, we hit an inadvertent homerun. Chuck and Ann really liked the life insurance plan. It seems that they had always been concerned that they might have financial responsibility for Julie's children if something happened to Ed.; but they had been reluctant to discuss this concern with Julie and Ed. So the fact that we had to purchase a large life insurance policy on Ed did not cause them to be concerned about the cost, but rather gave them additional financial security.

Note that the use of life insurance as a college funding vehicle doesn't always work well because the cost of the insurance indeed reduces the overall return on investment. But it might work well when we have a well-off grandparent and a not-so-well-off parent as was the case in the example. If properly set up, an insurance-driven arrangement can preserve financial aid benefits for a student while still giving tax benefits to the higher income grandparent.

The case of Chuck and Ann Sample is important for several reasons. First, it shows the importance of getting clients to focus on benefits, not products. Often fees originally perceived to be too high will become acceptable because the product produces important benefits that the client really wants. The case also shows that sometimes multiple tools are required in developing a plan. And finally, it shows that different plans may be required based on the needs of different grandchildren.

Including the Family in the Family Scholarship Plan™

The college problem is getting so large today that its solution may be beyond the scope of an individual parent or an individual grandparent. But combining family resources can make a difference. One of the advantages of the family scholarship plan is that the "family" can be brought into play.

Grandpa Bill had a problem—not the kind of problem that most of us have, but one nonetheless where his generosity could have caused a family rift.

Bill has two children. The first, his daughter, is a doctor who married a professor at Cornell University. He believes that they are well prepared to send their two children, his grandchildren, to college even if the children choose not to go to Cornell:

"When I saw my granddaughter walking around the house in a Cornell t-shirt, I made a joke about how Cornell would be their college savings plan," said Grandpa Bill, "but my daughter assured me that they'd have enough tucked away by then so that their children could go wherever they wanted to go to college."

It's Bill's son that Bill is concerned about. "My son and his wife seem to do well financially," he said, "but I'm worried that they're not saving for college." Why? They each drive big BMW SUVs, live in a sprawling mansion, and just bought a new sailboat. "If I bring up college savings, they just brush it aside, saying that college is a long way off," remarked Bill.

Bill's concern is that his grandchildren might have unequal education opportunities. Fortunately for Bill, he has saved, and saved well, for his retirement and would like to put some of that money towards his grandchildren's education. However, he doesn't want to reward his son and daughter-in-law for their excessive lifestyle. "It's my son's children who will really need my financial help, but I don't want to alienate my daughter by creating a situation where she thinks that I don't care about her children, too," said Bill.

What should Bill do?

Our solution was to create a Family Scholarship Plan where Bill opened a qualified tuition plan (Section 529 Plan) for each of his four grandchildren. He deposited $10,000 into each of his grandchildren's accounts and told both his children the same thing:

> "I have set up a Family Scholarship Plan for each of your children. In order to keep the plan, you need to make periodic deposits into the account. At the end of the year, I will match your contributions dollar-for-dollar."

The beauty of this plan is that Bill will be giving as much as his children are willing to contribute, and it gives both his daughter and his son incentive to tuck money away. This "matching plan" went a long way to squelching any family fights and towards helping his grandchildren have the advantage of a college education.

As part of the process of helping Grandpa Bill design the right plan, we also contacted each of Bill's children to determine what benefits they desired in the plan, just as we did with Chuck and Ann's children. Each wanted to control his or her own investments and the distributions that would be withdrawn from them. To meet the parents' needs, we actually set up another 529 plan for each grandchild, resulting in each grandchild being the beneficiary of two plans, one owned by the parent, the other owned by Grandpa Bill. At the end of the year, each parent sends a copy of his annual plan statement to Grandpa Bill. Grandpa Bill then matches the deposit in the parent-owned plan by depositing an equal amount into his plan. In this way, each plan owner is able to control his own plan.

There were several strategic byproducts that came out of this planning process. First, Grandpa Bill was so happy that he had a solution to his problem that he gave us a substantial amount of his other money to invest. Second, we wound up with two additional clients, Grandpa Bill's two children. One of the beauties of college planning is that it often results in an indirect referral to another generation.

More Intergenerational Referrals

There are other ways of bringing the family into the Family Scholarship Plan. One interesting slant on the process began when we worked with a set of young parents who set up a Family Scholarship Plan. These parents quickly realized that they were not going to be able to get a significant amount of money into the plan because they had high living expenses and limited resources. So they decided to include other family members in the savings process. They prepared a letter from their kids to other family members requesting donations to the Family Scholarship Plan. Here is the gist of the letter:

Dear Grandpa and Grandma,

Mommy and Daddy recently set up a Family Scholarship Plan™ so that I would have the opportunity to go to college. You have been extremely generous to me at Christmas and birthdays. Instead of giving me so many presents would you consider taking some of the money and putting it into my Family Scholarship Plan™ so I can go to an even better college?

Thank you.

Child's Name

Although this letter is rather hokey, and it is quickly obvious to grandparents that their grandchildren didn't really write the letter, they realize the importance of college savings, and often make significant contributions as a result of receiving the letter. All it takes is someone getting the plan started and someone inviting the family to participate. A recent study by OppenheimerFunds, Inc. revealed that parents and grandparents spend significantly more on toys and gifts than they do on saving money for college. Redirecting savings of grandparents can often be achieved simply by showing leadership. Setting up a Family Scholarship Plan and informing the family about the plan can often result in significant dollars flowing into the plan.

A Story of Two Dentists

The benefit of helping parents pay for college far transcends the commissions earned from the investments in a college savings account. College planning is just the beginning—it leads to retirement planning, estate planning, and intergenerational referrals. Do you remember the husband and wife dentist couple mentioned in the

Preface? We helped the dentists' parents get them through college and dental school. When the dentists were expecting a child of their own, their parents reminded them about the crisis they found themselves facing when the dentists were ready to go to college. Their parents' advice was, "Don't let yourselves get into the same kind of crunch, start saving right away and be consistent with it."

Their parents also strongly urged them to seek out our advice in designing their college savings plans. Today, the college savings plan for the dentists is in place, their second child has been born, their plan adjusted, and now we are also helping them start-up their own dental practice and create their own retirement plans.

When we started building this niche market, intergenerational prospecting didn't occur to us. However, it has become been a very satisfying strategic byproduct for growing our practice.

MORE COLLEGE SAVINGS PLAN IDEAS

The Pizza Money Plan

Mort and Sylvia were retired and living nicely on their pension and social security income. They didn't have a lot of money, but they did have about $100,000 divided up among four bank certificates of deposit as their security blanket. They didn't need the interest for their living expenses, but they weren't comfortable with the idea of not having that nest egg.

Mort and Sylvia have a grandson already in college and they wanted to help out while keeping within their limited budget. We suggested that since Mort and Sylvia didn't use the interest they earned on the CDs, to consider giving some of that interest to their grandson to help with his spending money – "pizza money" as many parents call it.

So they changed the arrangements at the bank to have a check issued each month to their grandson for the interest on one of the CDs. They purchased a funny greeting card and a self-addressed, stamped postcard as well. Inside the card they wrote:

"Grandpa and I didn't need this money this month and thought it would help you out at college. Have fun, and by the way, please take a minute to jot us a note on the enclosed postcard and let us know how you're doing."

So for the next several months, they sent the cards and checks to their grandson and got the reply postcard in the mail from him. Mort and Sylvia were thoroughly enjoying the experience. They felt like they were contributing, and the return post cards fostered a bonding relationship with their grandson.

After about six months we got a call from Sylvia saying, "We didn't get a post-card back. What do we do?" At my suggestion they sent the card and the postcard, but without a check. It's amazing how fast the postcards came flying back.

Mort and Sylvia didn't have a lot of money to work with, but they found a creative way to help with college and build a bond with their grandson. Had they paid something toward the tuition bill, it would have been appreciated, but sending monthly spending money made a much bigger impression on their grandson.

The Stock Option Plan

Michael was an attorney who had sold a successful practice some years back to take a job with the new administration in Washington, D.C. During the years he attended Ivy League schools, for both his undergraduate and law school, he had met and become friendly with the newly-elected President of the United States and was now going to work in the new administration. He strongly believed that this new opportunity came about as a result of the contacts he had made while in school.

However, this new opportunity came at a cost. His new salary was in the low six figures, a 50% reduction from his private practice income. In addition, he and his family had to relocate and buy a new home in suburban Virginia that was much more expensive than the one they sold to move there. For the ensuing eight years, Michael relished the new political connections he made and thoroughly enjoyed working on projects of national importance. Meanwhile, he wasn't making much progress on his financial goals.

Eight years later, the administration changed and because of his political connections Michael found a job in the private sector. He became the president of a small public corporation, earning $350,000 annually. A generous stock option plan was also part of his compensation package. Michael's wife felt it was time to get a serious plan in place for college now because they finally had the money.

Michael and his wife had two children, ages 9 and 12. Because Michael believed that his career successes were a direct result of the contacts he had made while in college and law school, Michael was adamant that his children would attend Ivy League-types of schools as well. His plan was to cash in his stock options when it came time to pay the college bills. We pointed out that there were several pitfalls to this plan:

1. When the president of a publicly traded company sells stock, it tends to depress the price of the stock, and the shareholders tend to get very unhappy about that. This is especially true when the stock is narrowly traded, as his was.

2.   Cashing in stock options will result in a large tax bill, so Michael will have to cash in additional stock options to cover the cost of the taxes as well as the college bills.

3.   What happens to his plan if the options are "out-of-the-money" when he needs to sell?

Our solution for Michael was relatively simple. We approached the Human Resource Director of his company with a plan for an orderly liquidation of his stock options. Then we would put the proceeds into a 529 college savings plan to take advantage of tax-deferred growth and potentially tax-free withdrawals if used for college expenses. This arrangement solved all of the problems. It worked for three reasons:

1.   By having an organized plan, it was explained to the shareholders that this was simply a plan to liquidate stocks to save for college. In addition, spreading the stock sales over time, in small increments, limited the depressive effect on the stock price.

2.   Tax-free is always better than taxable. Michael understood that by cashing in the options now and paying the taxes, he could put the money into a 529 college savings plan and get tax-deferred growth. Furthermore, if the proceeds are used for qualified education expenses, the growth could end up being totally tax-free!

3.   Cashing in the options periodically would mitigate the potential trap of the options being "out-of-the-money" when college bills start coming in.

This was a win-win situation for everyone. The corporation was happy because potential shareholder problems were avoided. Michael's wife was happy because she could see a tangible savings plan instead of relying on abstract investments like stock options. And Michael was happy because now he had a plan with tax benefits and knew what to do going forward.

Many executives have stock options and/or deferred bonus plans. Although these plans may defer taxes, they may not be the best way to save for college.

As a postscript to this story: we received a call from Michael about a year after we started his college plan saying he had lost his job with the company. He had 90 days to exercise his remaining stock options and the stock options were currently out of the money. Michael was happy that he had been able to capitalize on some of the options before this happened.

The "Me, Too" Plan

Section 529 plans are not just for kids. In fact, there is no age limit on who can have a 529 plan. Senior citizens who want to take courses and learn about things that interest them can reap 529 plan benefits as can middle age adults who may wish to pursue a second career. As seniors live longer, the opportunity for us to market continuing learning to seniors will grow. Community colleges will be some of the first to market accredited courses that meet the qualified tuition standards required to withdraw 529 plan monies tax-free. Best of all, seniors can hand down unused funds in 529 plans to their children and grandchildren with minimal tax consequences. However, gift tax and generation-skipping transfer tax apply to a transfer by reason of a change in the 529 plan beneficiary if the new beneficiary is in a lower generation than the old beneficiary or is not a member of the family of the old beneficiary. The following couple is already taking advantage of the opportunity:

Jim and Anne are both 59 years old. Jim plans to retire at age 60 because he has been offered a good buy-out by his employer. Anne expects to continue working to age 62. Both pursued technical majors in college and didn't have much of an opportunity to take courses in arts and literature. One of their goals is to take college-level courses in subjects that interest them. Jim and Anne also want to travel, something they curtailed while raising their family. But they don't want to just go lie on a beach somewhere; they want to travel and learn. Finally, Jim and Anne want to be able to help with college for all of their grandchildren. Education was very important to them. They feel it is what gave them a good life and will continue to provide them the opportunity to enjoy a comfortable lifestyle in retirement. They would like their grandchildren to have the same opportunities.

Jim has already begun investigating college courses at the local community college and he has discovered some courses that include some interesting field trips relating to the subject matter. He and Anne have each invested in their own 529 plan. They plan on paying for those learning experiences by making withdrawals from their respective 529 plans. Jim's CPA has indicated that as long as the course is a legitimate, accredited course offered by an institution that is eligible to participate in a student aid program administered by the U.S. Department of Education, withdrawals used to pay for qualified education expenses should be tax-free. Furthermore, at a later date, Jim and Anne can change the beneficiary on their plans to their grandchildren; but the CPA advised them to check with him on potential gift and generation-skipping taxes before making beneficiary changes.

THE "REAL" GRANDPARENT CONTRIBUTION™

A number of the stories above involve grandparents helping with college costs. If college costs continue to climb, as we expect they will, the grandparent contribution will be even more significant. Any contribution, whether a lump sum up front, an annual savings contribution, or even "Pizza Money Plan" will help. But the biggest contribution comes from getting dollars into the college plan *early* to take advantage of the compounded, often tax-free growth, afforded by today's college planning tools.

Parents usually don't have the ability to put larger sums into the college plan early, but grandparents often do. Trying to get lump sums into the plan early to take advantage of tax-free growth can make the difference in the success of a college savings plan. Even if a grandparent makes contributions into the plan early, and the parent pays the grandparent back later with dollars the parent would have contributed, the plan will probably end up with more money in it.

Sometimes, however, grandparents need to be motivated to help. They need to see that their contribution can be magnified significantly by compounded growth. The following example shows what we mean:

Grandpa and Grandma Thompson have decided to contribute $10,000 this year to a college plan for their grandson Tommy (age 2). In addition, they plan to add $10,000 each year for the next four years. They want to see what impact their savings would have on an Ivy League education for their grandson, Tommy who will enter college in 2024.

Data from Figure 2.3 shows that four years at an Ivy League college (Harvard) is estimated to cost about $714,000. Although the Thompson's contributions of $50,000 are only about 7% of the total college cost estimate, the investment growth at an assumed 7.5% compounded rate of return will add an additional $98,719 to the college account, or almost 14% more of the estimated college bill. Therefore, their "Real Contribution" to Tommy's college costs totals $148,719 or almost 21% of the estimated college bill.

Should Tommy attend a state college as an in-state resident (Rutgers in New Jersey), which is estimated to cost almost $311,000, the Thompson's $50,000 contribution plus approximately $105,000 of investment growth will pay 50% of the total bill. See Figure 2.4 for the illustration.

Figures 2.3 and 2.4 demonstrate the impact that grandparents can have with a college savings plan. But it is important to remind grandparents that whether they do a little or a lot, everything is greatly appreciated.

Figure 2.3 Ivy League College

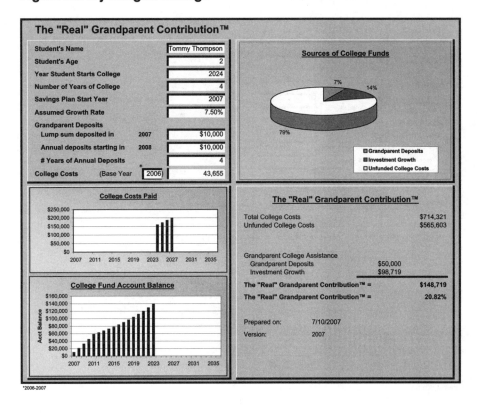

The "Real" Grandparent Contribution™

Student's Name	Tommy Thompson
Student's Age	2
Year Student Starts College	2024
Number of Years of College	4
Savings Plan Start Year	2007
Assumed Growth Rate	7.50%

Grandparent Deposits

Lump sum deposited in	2007	$10,000
Annual deposits starting in	2008	$10,000
# Years of Annual Deposits		4
College Costs (Base Year	2006)	43,655

Sources of College Funds

7%
14%
79%

☐ Grandparent Deposits
☐ Investment Growth
☐ Unfunded College Costs

College Costs Paid

The "Real" Grandparent Contribution™

Total College Costs		$714,321
Unfunded College Costs		$565,603
Grandparent College Assistance		
Grandparent Deposits	$50,000	
Investment Growth	$98,719	
The "Real" Grandparent Contribution™ =		$148,719
The "Real" Grandparent Contribution™ =		20.82%

Prepared on:	7/10/2007
Version:	2007

College Fund Account Balance

*2006-2007

Figure 2.4 State College (In-State Student)

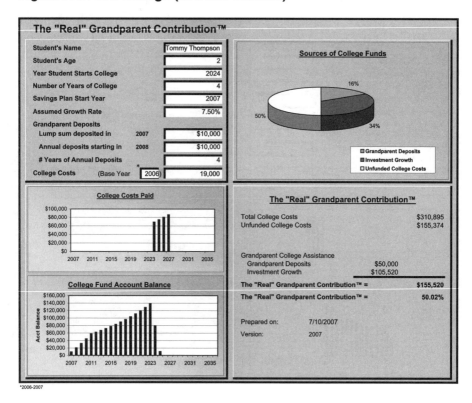

The "Real" Grandparent Contribution™

Student's Name	Tommy Thompson
Student's Age	2
Year Student Starts College	2024
Number of Years of College	4
Savings Plan Start Year	2007
Assumed Growth Rate	7.50%
Grandparent Deposits	
Lump sum deposited in 2007	$10,000
Annual deposits starting in 2008	$10,000
# Years of Annual Deposits	4
College Costs (Base Year 2006)	19,000

Sources of College Funds: 16%, 34%, 50%
- Grandparent Deposits
- Investment Growth
- Unfunded College Costs

The "Real" Grandparent Contribution™

Total College Costs	$310,895
Unfunded College Costs	$155,374

Grandparent College Assistance
Grandparent Deposits $50,000
Investment Growth $105,520
The "Real" Grandparent Contribution™ = $155,520
The "Real" Grandparent Contribution™ = 50.02%

Prepared on: 7/10/2007
Version: 2007

*2006-2007

Chapter 3

THE COLLEGE PLANNING PROCESS

The major differential in planning for college comes from different time horizons. Starting to plan before high school begins (**Long-Term Savings**) is quite different than starting to plan after high school begins (**Crisis Planning**). In addition, the person who initiates the planning process also makes a difference in how the plan is constructed. For example, a grandparent has more planning considerations to analyze than a parent, since many times the grandparent is dealing with multiple families having different financial circumstances. This chapter will lay out the key tasks that need to be completed for a successful college plan. The table below summarizes the four different processes that we will investigate.

College Planning Processes		
	Long-Term Planning Time Horizon	**Short-Term Planning Time Horizon**
Parent-Initiated Planning	**1** Long-Term Savings Plan	**2** Crisis Plan
Grandparent/Other Person-Initiated Planning	**3** Long-Term Savings Plus	**4** Crisis Planning Plus

In this chapter, we will diagram and describe each step of each process and give a specific case study showing how we attack the problem using tools from Chapters 6, 7, and 8.

PARENT-INITIATED LONG-TERM SAVINGS PLANS

There are four distinct planning steps shown in Figure 3.1 that are a part of a parent-initiated long term savings plan. They include:

- *The Diagnostic Step* – designed to capture college planning goals and document the resources that a family is willing to devote to college. This is usually an iterative process. Parents often underestimate college costs and may need to rethink college goals. It is also important during this phase to make sure that parents understand that college and retirement are linked, and that committing resources to college will impact their ability to retire.

- *The Plan Design Step* – structured to finalize planning goals and funding commitments as a result of the discussion in the diagnostic stage. Appropriate generic tools such as 529 plans, Coverdell Education Savings Accounts (ESAs), etc., also are selected.

- *The Implementation Step* – designed to choose specific tools (i.e., which state's 529 plan, which mutual funds within the plan, what asset allocation, etc.). Paperwork to get the plan started is completed during this phase and accounts are opened.

- *The Monitoring Step* – planned to arrange annual follow up meetings; designed to note changes in family circumstances and changes in external factors that would impact the college plan (e.g., financial aid). Plans need to be adjusted to compensate for changes. Most important is monitoring retirement plan adequacy.

Figure 3.1 Parent-Initiated Long-Term Savings Plans

Planning Steps	Overview
Diagnostics	Document the Client's Goals & Circumstances
Plan Design	Finalize Plan Targets & Choose the Appropriate Tools
Implementation	Choose the Specific Financial Vehicles
Monitoring	Annual Meeting to Adjust for Changes & Coordinate with Retirement Goals

Figures 3.2, 3.3, 3.4, and 3.5 breakdown each of the major planning steps into generic sub-steps and also indicate College Money's specific tools that may be helpful in planning. We discuss each of these College Money specific tools in Chapters 6, 7, and 8. Examples of how they are used appear throughout the text.

The **Diagnostic Step** (Figure 3.2) consists of four generic sub-steps:

1. *Explore college costs and set realistic goals.* A great way to set goals is to have the College Planning Conversation™ with your client. It is an easy way to help the client to get a grip on college costs, college inflation, and the impact that college costs can have on his retirement plans.

2. *Define the most important plan features.* The Family Scholarship Plan™ graphic will help your client focus on the important features and benefits that he can derive from a properly structured college plan. The Benefits Evaluator Form™ will help you prioritize the clients' feelings and later match them with the appropriate planning tools.

3. *Determine if financial aid will likely play an important role in the planning process.* Everyone would like to get help from the financial aid system to pay college bills. The Financial Aid Test™ and the Financial Aid Appraisal™ are two tools that can help determine if financial aid should be considered a significant factor in the planning process or if it should be bypassed as not a realistic consideration.

4. *Evaluate the current plan and the parent commitment to funding the current plan.* Understanding the current college savings plan, if one exists, can help the advisor formulate a better one. One can ascertain what is working and what is not. An advisor can also get an understanding of the client's current commitment to college. Including the current plan balances in the College Planning Conversation will show the client any shortcomings in his plan and again demonstrate the impact it will have on his retirement plan.

The **Plan Design Step** consists of two sub-steps as shown in Figure 3.3:

1. *Identify the appropriate generic funding vehicles.* By this we mean should we use a 529 plan, an ESA, variable life insurance, etc. There are a couple of tools available to provide assistance. In the Diagnostics Step we completed The Benefits Evaluation Form™ to tabulate and prioritize the client's feelings about important features to build into his college plan. Matching data from that form to the College Planning

Figure 3.2 Parent-Initiated Long-term Savings Plans
Diagnostics

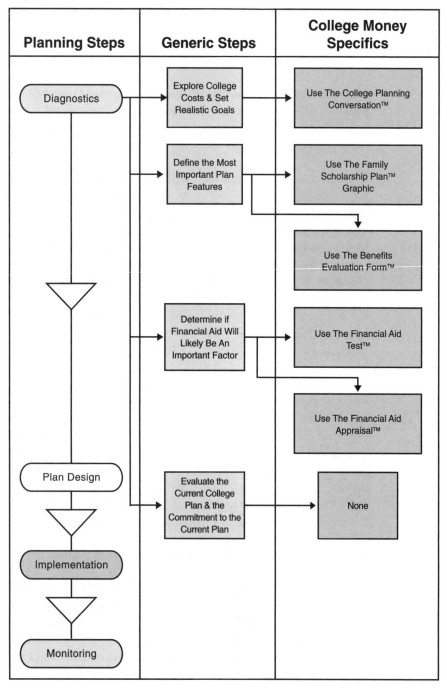

Figure 3.3 Parent-Initiated Long-term Savings Plans
Plan Design

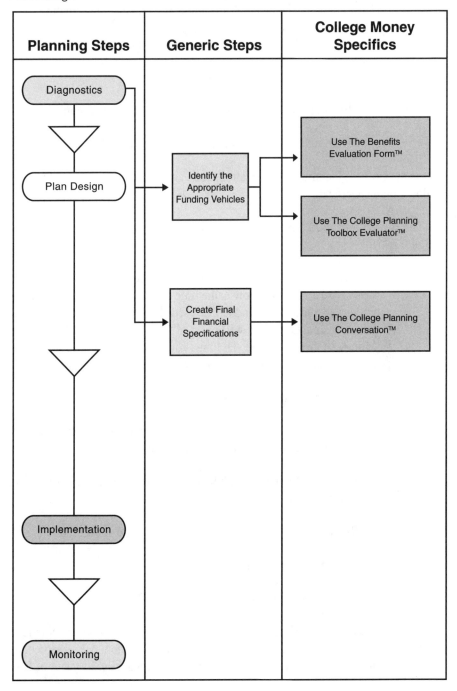

Tool/Benefits Grid™ can help choose the appropriate saving tools. It is important to note that both of these tools are somewhat subjective. They are meant to be a helpful guide, not an absolute selection tool.

2.   Create the final financial specifications for the plan.

- How much will the client save each year?

- How much of a lump sum will he deposit into the plan?

- When will the college debts be totally paid off?

Having the College Planning Conversation, once again, is an effective tool to help pin down plan specifications.

The **Implementation Step** consists of three sub-steps which are summarized in Figure 3.4:

1.   *Choose the specific plan funding vehicle.* If the decision in Plan Design was to use a 529 plan, now is the time to choose which state plan and which specific mutual fund will be used? If variable life was the choice, which insurance carrier will be used? We offer no specific College Money tools to use here. Helping your client find the right funding product needs to be based on your experience and knowledge.

<u>A few suggestions on choosing a 529 plan</u>

- Look first at the client's state of residence. Often there are tax advantages associated with an in-state plan.

- Carefully review the offering statement for any plan you are considering.

- To help evaluate performance data two good sources are:

  - www.morningstar.com

  - www.savingforcollege.com

2.   *Set the asset allocation.* We have no specific tools that are unique to college when it comes to setting an asset allocation. Advisors need to note that the college time horizon is short, usually 20 years or less.

Figure 3.4 The Parent-Initiated Long-term Savings Plans
Implementation

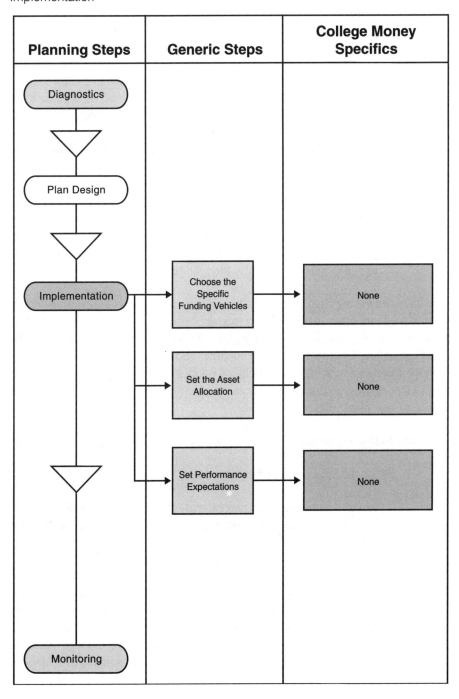

Planning Steps	Generic Steps	College Money Specifics
Diagnostics		
Plan Design		
Implementation	Choose the Specific Funding Vehicles	None
	Set the Asset Allocation	None
	Set Performance Expectations	None
Monitoring		

Many advisors use an age-based asset allocation adjustment generally starting aggressively when children are young and getting conservative as college approaches.

3. *Set the performance expectations.* We find it helpful to discuss performance expectations with the client so that when we conduct periodic reviews, the client will know when it is appropriate to make a change. Usually we develop a composite benchmark to act as a guide to us and to the client. For example, we might compare fund performance for an 80% stock, 20% bond portfolio to a composite benchmark of 80% Wilshire 5000 Index and 20% Lehman Bond Index. This section is not meant to be an in-depth discussion of performance evaluation, and each advisor needs to develop a system of his or her own. The most important thing is to do something. Clients often want to know if they should be changing college funding vehicles. Because of the short college planning time horizon and the fact that college funding products are not as liquid as other financial vehicles, making changes to a plan must be carefully thought through.

The **Monitoring Step** (Figure 3.5) is often overlooked because college plans, when started, are often small. This is a mistake. As college gets closer the pressure builds on parents. Contributions will increase if you, the advisor, stay on top of the client's situation. Grandparents will sometimes add dollars. The advisor who stays in touch can do great things for his clients by making them pay attention to their plan. A strategic by-product of the annual college-planning meeting is also another chance to take over the retirement plan.

The **Monitoring Step** has three main sub-steps shown in Figure 3.5:

1. Set up the annual monitoring meeting.

2. Review family changes and external changes that can affect the college plan. Changes in income, number of family members, etc., can change the dynamics of the college plan. New planning tools, changes in financial aid rules, or new legislation can also make a difference.

3. Rerun the **Diagnostics** and amend the plan. Two tools should be used at least annually. Rerunning the Financial Aid Test will automatically update family financials. Because financial aid can be so important to a plan, it needs to be monitored. Finally, the College Planning Conversation will often motivate parents to increase plan deposit commitments.

Figure 3.5 The Parent-Initiated Long-term Savings Plans
Monitoring

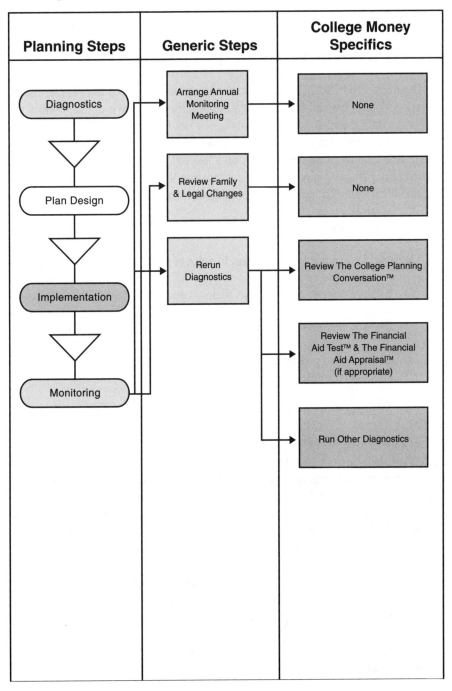

CASE STUDY

To help clarify the preceding process, the Scott Family Case Study has been designed to demonstrate how the process and tools can help a client.

The Scott Family: Long-Term Savings Plans

Dean and Linda Scott, both 36-years-old, met as undergraduates at Dartmouth University. Linda has put her career as a marketing executive on hold while she stays home with their two children, Amy (age 4) and Danny (age 1). Amy will start college in 2021 and Danny will follow 3 years later in 2024. Dean is currently employed as an industrial engineer and is on a fast track with his company. Dean and Linda recently finished paying off their education loans and would like to redirect that money now to a college savings plan for their children.

Step 1: The Diagnostic Step

There are four major tasks we want to achieve during the diagnostic step:

1. Explore college costs and set realistic goals.

2. Choose the benefits most desirable to the family in their college plan.

3. Explore the feasibility of getting future financial aid and evaluating its effect on the college plan.

4. Evaluate the current college plan if the family has already started one.

We began by having the College Planning Conversation with Dean and Linda to learn what their current goals are and how they hope to achieve them. Their immediate response was that they hoped that both children would go to Dartmouth as they did. They admitted though, that they have no idea how much it costs to go to Dartmouth today, much less what it would cost them 14 years from now. Using the College Planning Conversation (Figure 3.6), we demonstrated what their college costs would be and helped them quantify their initial plan.

The bar chart imbedded in Figure 3.6 shows the projected college bill (based on 2006-2007 costs) for each year that the Scotts will have a student in college. In 2021, the Scotts will need a little over $125,000 for Amy's first year. In 2024, the Scotts will have two students in college at the same time. The anticipated bill that year will exceed $315,000 for their two children. The Scotts' total college cost will approximate $1,200,000.

Figure 3.6

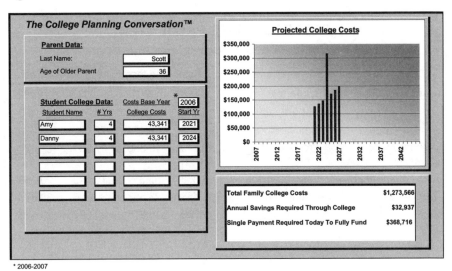

The College Planning Conversation™

Parent Data:

Last Name:	Scott
Age of Older Parent	36

Student College Data:

Student Name	# Yrs	College Costs	Start Yr
Amy	4	43,341	2021
Danny	4	43,341	2024

Costs Base Year* 2006

Projected College Costs

Total Family College Costs	$1,273,566
Annual Savings Required Through College	$32,937
Single Payment Required Today To Fully Fund	$368,716

* 2006-2007

The first stumbling block we ran into was that the Scotts simply could not believe that four years at an Ivy League school for two children could possibly cost over a million dollars. To help them understand that this scenario is highly likely, we had them look at what college costs today along with college inflation rates.

Figure 3.7 shows the projected college costs that underlie the college costs projections in Figure 3.6. We asked the Scotts to note the cost of Dartmouth ($43,341) for the school year 2006 - 2007. This is the real cost, right now. This means that if Amy and Danny were attending Dartmouth now, four years of college would cost about $210,000 each, or $421,000 for both.

We then showed the Scotts the average inflation figures for college inflation and CPI as seen in Figure 3.8. Since college inflation has consistently outpaced CPI by about a 2-to-1 margin, this factor started to bring things a little more into focus for them. As an engineer, Dean quickly noted that with a college inflation rate of more than 5% per year, he could now see how costs would more than double over the next 14 years. Seeing these numbers and doing the simple math helped Dean and Linda to grasp the magnitude of future college costs.

Note: It was extremely important to get the Scotts to buy into the college cost projections *before* proceeding. We could, if necessary, go on Dartmouth's website to show current college costs. Without the Scott's buy-in, there is no use in continuing since we would not have the credibility necessary and the Scotts would not have the motivation to later implement the plan.

Figure 3.7

COLLEGE COSTS PROJECTED
Yearly Tuition, Fees, Supplies, Room & Board

Name of Institution	Location	Assuming Increases of 5% Per Year			
		2007	**2012**	**2017**	**2022**
Auburn University	Auburn, Ala.	14,172	18,087	23,085	29,463
Bowdoin College	Brunswick, Maine	44.750	57,114	72,893	93,032
Brigham Young University	Provo, Utah	10,640	13,580	17,331	22,120
Bucknell University	Lewisburg, Pa.	43,368	55,350	70,642	90,159
The Citadel	Charleston, S.C.	18,458	23,558	30,066	38,373
Colorado State University	Ft. Collins, Colo.	12,706	16,216	20,697	26,415
Columbia College	New York, N.Y.	44,814	57,195	72,997	93,165
Dartmouth College	Hanover, N.H.	43,341	55,315	70,598	90,103
De Paul University	Chicago, Ill.	33,085	42,226	53,892	68,781
Drake University	Des Moines, Iowa	29,182	37,244	47,534	60,667
Duke University	Durham, N.C.	46,050	58,773	75,011	95,735
Emory University	Atlanta, Ga.	43,444	55,447	70,766	90,317
Florida State University	Tallahassee, Fla.	11,385	14,530	18,545	23,669
George Washington Univ.	Washington, D.C.	50,420	64,350	82,129	104,820
Hamline University	St. Paul, Minn.	33,312	42,515	54,262	69,253
Harvard College	Cambridge, Mass.	43,655	55,716	71,109	90,756
Jackson State University	Jackson, Miss.	8,976	11,456	14,621	18,660
Kansas State University	Manhattan, Kans.	12,246	15,629	19,947	25,459
Loyola College in Maryland	Baltimore, Md.	41,825	53,380	68,129	86,951
Marquette University	Milwaukee, Wis.	34,094	43,514	55,536	70,879
Michigan State University	E. Lansing, Mich.	15,784	20,145	25,710	32,814
Middlebury College	Middlebury, Vt.	45,570	58,160	74,229	94,737
Ohio State University	Columbus, Ohio	15,903	20,297	25,904	33,061
Oral Roberts University	Tulsa, Okla.	24,930	31,818	40,608	51,828
Purdue University	W. Lafayette, Ind.	14,268	18,210	23,241	29,662
Rutgers College	New Brunswick, N.J.	19,000	24,249	30,949	39,500
St. Lawrence University	Canton, N.Y.	42,530	54,280	69,277	88,417
Salem International Univ.	Salem, W.Va.	18,920	24,147	30,819	39,333

Seattle University	Seattle, Washington	32,598	41,604	53,099	67,769
Southern Methodist Univ.	Dallas, Tex.	41,705	53,227	67,933	86,702
Stanford University	Stanford, Calif.	45,046	57,491	73,375	93,647
Texas A & M University	College Sta., Tex.	15,905	20,299	25,908	33,065
Tulane University	New Orleans, La.	44,093	56,275	71,823	91,666
University of Arkansas	Fayetteville, Ark.	13,286	16,957	21,641	27,621
University of California	Berkley, Calif.	22,200	28,333	36,161	46,152
University of Louisville	Louisville, Ky.	12,148	15,504	19,788	25,255
University of New Mexico	Albuquerque, N.Mex.	12,236	15,617	19,931	25,438
University of Rhode Island	Kingston, R.I.	18,092	23,090	29,470	37,612
University of Virginia	Charlottesville, Va.	15,944	20,349	25,971	33,146
Vanderbilt University	Nashville, Tenn.	45,434	57,987	74,007	94,454
Yale University	New Haven, Conn.	45,850	58,518	74,685	95,319
Yeshiva University	New York, N.Y.	37,370	47,695	60,872	77,690
Average Cost		**29,018**	**37,035**	**47,266**	**60,325**

Explanation of Table. Costs for public schools assume the student is a resident of the state. Costs (i.e., tuition) for out-of-state students are generally substantially more then shown. Costs for supplies are included when available. Costs for transportation and other costs (e.g., networking or "pizza" money) are not included. Since over the past decade college costs have more than kept pace with the rate of inflation, it seems highly likely that costs will continue to escalate in the years to come.

Source: Cady, *2007 Field Guide to Estate Planning, Business Planning, & Employee Benefits,* page 112 (Cincinnati, OH: The National Underwriter Company, 2007).

Our next step was to ask the Scotts how they planned to accomplish those goals. Linda handles the family finances so she volunteered that they have already saved about $10,000 for college, and the monthly payment they were making to pay off their education loans was $400 ($4,800 annually). Using that as a starting point, Linda felt they could make a monthly savings deposit of $500 for college ($6,000 annually). As a disciplined saver, Linda added that she planned to increase her savings by 5% per year in order to stay close to college inflation. Linda had obviously gotten the message about college inflation. She estimated that by the time college starts, they would be putting about $12,000 a year toward college. She thought that during the college years, they could stretch payments to $15,000 annually. Figure 3.9 illustrates the results of Linda's plan.

The upswing on the graph in Figure 3.9 represents the **savings period**. Based on Linda's plans, the Scotts' savings would accumulate to a little more than $211,000

Figure 3.8: A History of College Inflation vs. CPI

Year	College Inflation	CPI	Difference
Average	**8.08%**	**4.15%**	**3.93%**
2006	7.06%	3.82%	3.24%
2005	7.33%	3.64%	3.69%
2004	8.43%	2.65%	5.78%
2003	9.53%	2.16%	7.37%
2002	7.10%	1.80%	5.30%
2001	5.64%	2.72%	2.92%
2000	4.26%	3.41%	0.85%
1999	3.94%	2.26%	1.68%
1998	3.89%	1.62%	2.27%
1997	5.12%	2.23%	2.89%
1996	5.71%	2.88%	2.83%
1995	6.39%	2.62%	3.77%
1994	7.24%	2.90%	4.34%
1993	9.32%	2.77%	6.55%
1992	11.43%	3.15%	8.28%
1991	8.74%	3.80%	4.94%
1990	9.17%	5.62%	3.55%
1989	7.82%	4.71%	3.11%
1988	8.40%	4.02%	4.38%
1987	8.74%	4.28%	4.46%
1986	8.36%	1.57%	6.79%
1985	9.33%	3.35%	5.98%
1984	10.29%	4.29%	6.00%
1983	10.58%	2.56%	8.02%
1982	14.01%	5.85%	8.16%
1981	12.23%	10.80%	1.43%
1980	8.19%	12.87%	-4.68%
1979	7.99%	11.82%	-3.83%

Source - CPI Data: U.S. Department Of, Bureau of Labor Statistics, Consumer Price Index, All Urban Consumers - (CPI-U), U.S. city average All items, 1982-84=100, September 1 to August 31
Source - College Inflation CPI-U, College Tuition and Fees

Figure 3.9

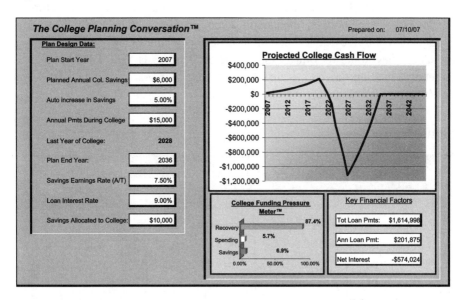

by the year Amy starts college. The downward sloping line represents the **spending and borrowing period**. During this period, they would pay $15,000 per year out of current income and would dip into their college savings. By Danny's freshman year, the Scotts will have depleted their savings and will have to borrow to supplement the annual payment of $15,000 from current income. When college is over for both children, Dean and Linda will have borrowed approximately $1,100,000. Because the Scotts want to retire in 2036, they would have a very short **recovery period** (the period of time between the end of college and the beginning of retirement), and would have to make annual loan payments of $201,875 during the **recovery period** in order to be out of debt by their regular retirement age.

Recalling that the dual purpose of the College Planning Conversation is to educate parents about college costs *and* clearly demonstrate the link between college and retirement, we allowed a minute to pass in order for Dean and Linda to fully appreciate the impact of their plans. We then pointed out the huge dip in the graph that illustrated their borrowing. This is a clear picture of the retirement problem that they have created for themselves. At this point, Dean and Linda are pushing more than 87% of their college funding into the recovery period and they will not have much time until their planned retirement will start.

Satisfied that they finally understood the enormity of their goals, we suggested that they have two possible options to solve this retirement problem. First, they could divert more resources toward the college problem by saving more money now or paying more out of pocket later. Linda commented that she planned to return to the workforce once both children are in school, so that could help with the saving. Second, they could scale back their target costs for the time being. Once the children are older, they could reevaluate their target college costs then. Linda suggested targeting a medium-priced private college (Drake University). Figure 3.10 shows the difference this adjustment makes.

Figure 3.10

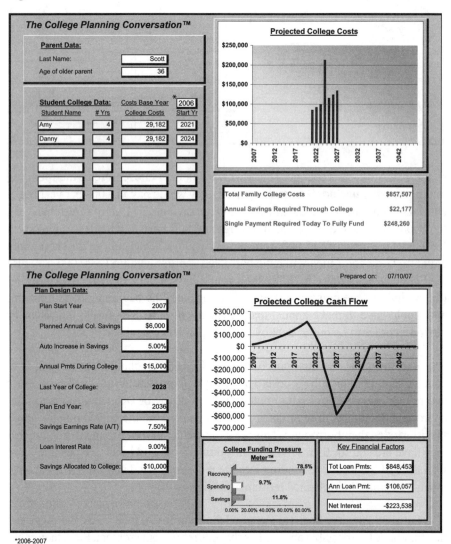

*2006-2007

Here is a comparison of the two plans. Note in the table below that they are still putting tremendous pressure on their retirement by borrowing heavily and pushing more than 78% of their funding into the recovery period.

						Spending	
	Total	Total	Total	Annual	Savings	&	Recovery
Plan	College	Amount	Loan	Loan	Period	Borrowing	Period
Iteration	Costs	Saved	Payments	Payments	%	Period %	%
1 Dartmouth	$1,273,566	$211,000	$1,614,998	$201,875	6.9%	5.7%	87.4%
2 Drake	$857,507	$211,000	$848,453	$106,057	11.8%	9.7%	78.5%

Plan Comparison A

Although there was a significant improvement, the numbers for a medium-priced college were still daunting to the Scotts. So we suggested saving for state college for an in-state student (Rutgers in New Jersey). This would guarantee at least a state college education for the Scotts' children. In the future, they could always change the plan based on what is happening in their lives and in the academic environment. The Scotts would also have the ability to commit more from current income during the college years. Linda is planning on returning to work. Figure 3.11 provides the final plan numbers. The third iteration is finally achieving some balance in the percentage allocations to the three college funding periods. The Scotts are now funding 24% in the saving period and just over 56% in the recovery period. Most important, loan payments during the recovery period are more manageable.

Figure 3.11

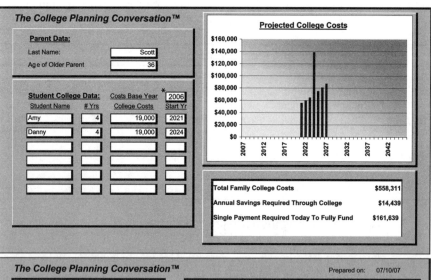

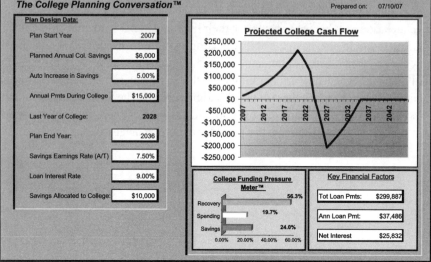

*2006-2007

The table below summarizes the three planning iterations we went through for the Scotts. At this point, they have a clear picture of their minimum college funding goals. They understand how important it is to meet their savings commitments. Linda knows that her future income is going to be required to bolster the college plan. She does not know, however, when she will go back to work and whether she will contribute to the savings component, the current income component, or both. The Scotts can now think about their commitment to college funding and perhaps redirect resources to enhance their plan. We will give them another chance to re-evaluate their funding plan in the design phase.

Plan Comparison B							
Plan Iteration	Total College Costs	Total Amount Saved	Total Loan Payments	Annual Loan Payments	Savings Period %	Spending & Borrowing Period %	Recovery Period %
1 Dartmouth	$1,273,566	$211,000	$1,614,998	$201,875	6.9%	5.7%	87.4%
2 Drake	$857,507	$211,000	$848,453	$106,057	11.8%	9.7%	78.5%
3 Rutgers	$558,311	$211,000	$299,887	$37,486	24.0%	19.7%	56.3%

The next step is to introduce **the Family Scholarship Plan**. You may recall that there are two components to the Family Scholarship Plan. The first component is getting the client to identify and understand the benefits that they would most like to build-in to their college savings plan. This will help us choose the right college funding tools. The second component, to be discussed later, is bringing the family into the college plan. We showed the following list of potential benefits to the Scotts. Then we asked them to talk to us about what they thought would be most important to them.

Dean and Linda reviewed the list and determined that because their expected income will grow quickly, tax-free growth will be extremely important in their savings plan. Distribution control is also a high priority because they do not want their children to have access to the money if they do not go to college. They were willing to cede investment control to the experts provided that they have periodic review. The only other feature they weren't quite sure about was potential financial aid. Clearly if it was going to be available to them, they wanted the help. However, they weren't sure how to evaluate that possibility.

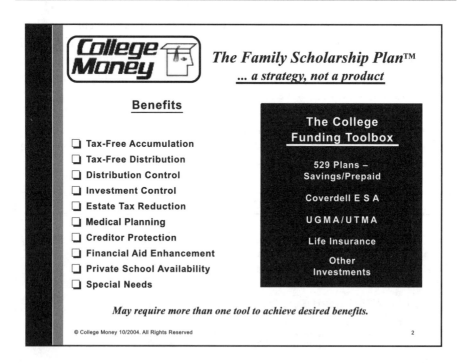

College Money 📖

The Family Scholarship Plan™
... a strategy, not a product

Benefits

- ❑ Tax-Free Accumulation
- ❑ Tax-Free Distribution
- ❑ Distribution Control
- ❑ Investment Control
- ❑ Estate Tax Reduction
- ❑ Medical Planning
- ❑ Creditor Protection
- ❑ Financial Aid Enhancement
- ❑ Private School Availability
- ❑ Special Needs

The College Funding Toolbox

529 Plans –
Savings/Prepaid

Coverdell E S A

U G M A / U T M A

Life Insurance

Other
Investments

May require more than one tool to achieve desired benefits.

© College Money 10/2004. All Rights Reserved   2

In order to help them, we performed a **Financial Aid Test** (Figure 3.12) to determine their **Parent Expected Contribution**. That, coupled with **the Financial Aid Appraisal** (Figures 3.13, 3.14, 3.15) gave us a picture of what percentage of college might be paid by the financial aid system in the future.

Initially, we explained to the Scotts that the Financial Aid Test looks at their income and assets as if their children were going to school *today*. The test calculates the parent and the family expected contributions that a college would expect them to pay towards college costs. Any difference represents potential financial aid. Although this early picture is a guess at best, it can give a feeling for whether or not to plan for aid. The Financial Aid Appraisal adds in such factors as increasing income and assets to help project results into the future.

The Scotts gave us the data we needed to handle the Financial Aid Test (Figure 3.12). We determined that if the Scotts' daughter, Amy, were attending a state college (Rutgers in New Jersey) as an in-state resident today, college costs would approximate $19,000 (see Figure 3.7). According to the Federal and Institutional Methodologies, the Scotts would be expected to pay $26,584 and $21,377 respectively, based on their current income and assets. Since the Scotts' ability to pay

(Parent Expected Contribution) is greater than the cost of college, they would not be eligible for financial aid (see below).

Scott Family Financial Aid Picture: One Student in College		
	Federal Methodology	**Institutional Methodology**
College Costs	$19,000	$19,000
Parent Expected Contribution	$26,584	$21,377
Financial Need	None	None

An exception occurs, however, when both of the Scott's children are in college at the same time. This occurs in only one year, 2024. In that year, college costs increase while parent resources do not increase proportionately. The table below shows how the Scott family would qualify for aid with two in college today (note that we do not show the corresponding Financial Aid Test results for this scenario). We explained to the Scotts that qualifying for financial aid does not mean that aid is guaranteed. Financial aid packages are college-dependent. That is to say, rich colleges might meet full financial need, while others might leave a gap. Packages may also contain loans or work/study. Not all is free money.

Scott Family Financial Aid Picture: Two Students in College		
	Federal Methodology	**Institutional Methodology**
College Costs	$38,000	$38,000
Parent Expected Contribution	$13,894	$13,087
Financial Need	$24,106	$24,913

The Financial Aid Appraisal (Figure 3.13) asks the client to make a few assumptions. The first assumption is an inflation figure (3.5%) and the second is how the clients expect their income to change with respect to that inflation factor. Two factors entered into the Scott's assumptions: (1) Dean is on a career fast-track

Figure 3.12

The Financial Aid Test™

Version 2007
01-Aug-07

Family Data:

Parent's Name (in report form)	Scott
Student's Name (in report form)	Danny
Street Address	9876 Main Street
City, State, ZIP	Passaic, NJ 01234
Home Telephone:	610-000-0000
Business Telephone:	215-000-0000
State of Residence (All Caps, e.g., NJ)	NJ
1 Age of Older Parent	36
2 Number of Parents in Family	2
3 Number of Dependent Children in Family	2
4 Number of Students in College for Plan Year	2
5 Total Ages of All Pre-college Children	0

Student Financial Data:

23 Student's Assets	$0
24 Student's Income	
a From Work	$0
b From Investments	$0
25 Student Income Tax Paid	$0
26 Assets in Siblings Names (IM only)	$0

Parent Financial Data:

6	Father's Wages	$99,000
7	Mother's Wages	$20,000
8	Other Taxable Income	$500
9	Nontaxable Income	$0
10	Untaxed Benefits	$0
11	Losses from Business, Farm, Capital Losses)	$0
12	Adjustments to Income	$0
13	Child Support Paid	$0
14	Tuition Tax Credits	$0
15	Taxable Student Aid	$0
16	Medical & Dental Expense	$3,500
17	Federal Income Taxes Paid	$8,000
18	Net Home Equity (include farm if you live on it)	
	a Market Value	$300,000
	b Sum of All Mortgages	$220,000
19	Net Equity of Other Real Estate	
	a Market Value	$0
	b Sum of All Mortgages	$0
20	Business/Farm Net Value (Your Share)	
	a Business Net Value	$0
	b Farm Net Value (if not used as residence)	$0
21	Parent Cash	$3,000
22	Parent Investments	
	a Qualified Retirement Plans	$143,500
	b Other	$5,000
	Debts Other Than Mortgages	$0

The Financial Aid Test™ - Quick Calc

Federal Methodology

Parent Expected Cont./Student	$13,894
Student Expected Contribution	$0
Expected Family Contribution/Student	$13,894

Key Counseling Numbers
Federal Methodology

	Assets	Income
% EPC From:	0.00%	100.00%
% ESC From:	0.00%	0.00%
Par. Marg.Cont.:	5.64%	47.00%
Stud. Marg. Cont:	20.00%	50.00%

Institutional Methodology

Parent Expected Cont./Student	$12,997
Student Expected Contribution	$1,550
Expected Family Contribution/Student	$14,547

Key Counseling Numbers
Institutional Methodology

	Assets	Income
% EPC From:	3.17%	96.83%
% ESC From:	0.00%	100.00%
Par. Marg. Cont:	3.00%	46.00%
Stud. Marg. Cont:	25.00%	50.00%

This analysis provides estimated financial aid data for planning purposes only. Actual financial aid awards are determined by each college at the time of admission. The validity of the input data can dramatically affect financial aid values. Which assets must be counted and how each asset is valued may be treated differently by the government and each individual college. Calculations are based on:
Federal Methodology   2007-08

Institutional Methodology 2007-08

Source: "CSS/Financial Aid PROFILE® User's Guide"

Copyright © 2007-08 The College Board, www.collegeboard.com.

Reproduced with permission.

The Institutional Methodology Worksheet and Computational Tables may be used by the individual purchaser of the CD but may not be posted on any website or reproduced in any other digital format without the express written consent of the College Board.

where he works and expects his income to increase faster than inflation; (2) Linda currently works part-time, but she expects to resume her career when the children are in school. To adjust for future income, the Scotts opted to state that their income would increase much faster than inflation for purposes of the analysis. The Scotts also expect to receive a lump sum inheritance of $198,000 in 2021.

The first Financial Aid Appraisal (Figure 3.13) confirmed that if the Scotts sent their children to state colleges as in-state residents, they would qualify for financial aid only in the years Danny is in college. But they were surprised to learn that aid might be worth as much as 16% of the college bill. We also performed two additional Financial Aid Appraisals for the Scotts at medium-priced private and Ivy League colleges (Figures 3.14 and 3.15, respectively). The salient data is summarized here.

Potential Financial Aid Summary			
	Total College Costs	Scott's Expected Contribution $	Potential Financial Aid $	Potential Financial Aid %
State College (in-state)	$558,311	$468,351	$89,960	16%
Private	$857,507	$481,217	$376,290	44%
Ivy League	$1,273,566	$481,217	$792,349	62%

The Scotts were encouraged to discover that if they opt for higher-priced colleges, financial aid might help. But they were also wary that even though the financial aid award might be significant, their potential contribution might also be higher than they could handle. Conservatively, they decided not to count on financial aid at this point in their planning, but instead to monitor financial aid eligibility as the college planning time horizon progressed.

Two observations about financial aid are important to the Scotts:

1.   Financial aid rules are likely to change over time. Therefore, it is wise for the Scotts not to count on financial aid.

2.   Financial aid can give the Scotts hope that their Ivy League school dreams may still be met.

Figure 3.13

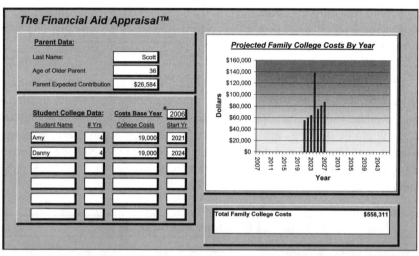

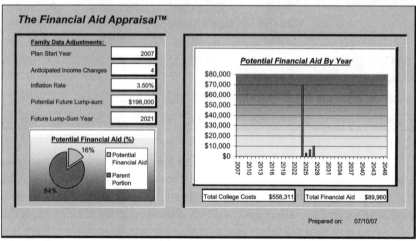

This program is designed to help families plan for future college expenditures. It projects future college costs and future financial aid eligibility based on current and past college cost data and current financial aid formulas which can change substantially over time. **This program is intended for planning purposes only and implies no guarantees.**

Projecting college costs and financial aid can be useful in the planning process to help decide on savings commitments and college funding vehicles. But for best results, projections should be recalculated annually using the most current version of this spreadsheet.

Version: 2007

*2006-2007

Figure 3.14

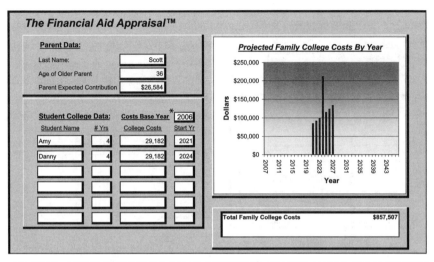

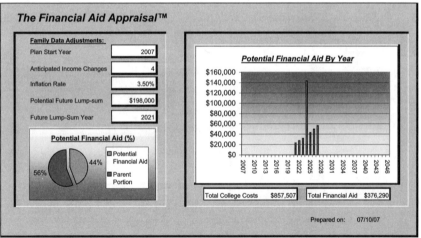

This program is designed to help families plan for future college expenditures. It projects future college costs and future financial aid eligibility based on current and past college cost data and current financial aid formulas which can change substantially over time. **This program is intended for planning purposes only and implies no guarantees.**

Projecting college costs and financial aid can be useful in the planning process to help decide on savings commitments and college funding vehicles. But for best results, projections should be recalculated annually using the most current version of this spreadsheet.

Version: 2007

*2006-2007

Figure 3.15

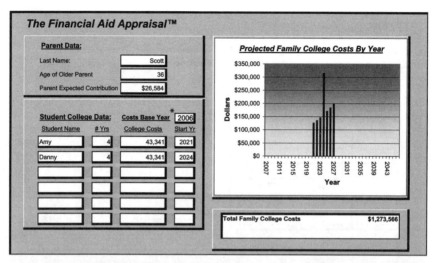

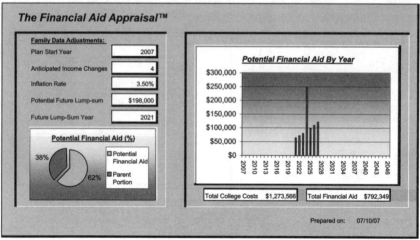

This program is designed to help families plan for future college expenditures. It projects future college costs and future financial aid eligibility based on current and past college cost data and current financial aid formulas which can change substantially over time. **This program is intended for planning purposes only and implies no guarantees.**

Projecting college costs and financial aid can be useful in the planning process to help decide on savings commitments and college funding vehicles. But for best results, projections should be recalculated annually using the most current version of this spreadsheet.

Version: 2007

*2006-2007

Based on our discussion of the Family Scholarship Plan with the Scotts, we were able to help them complete the Benefit Evaluation Form shown below. The form indicates the degree of importance the Scotts assigned to each benefit. It will help us choose the right planning tools to help the Scotts implement their plan.

Benefit Evaluation Form **The Family Scholarship Plan™**	**Ranking** 10 = Most Important 1 = Least Important
1 Tax-free growth	10
2 Tax-free distributions	10
3 Investment control	6
4 Distribution control	10
5 Estate planning	1
6 Creditor protection	1
7 Medical planning	1
8 Ability to pay for private elementary and secondary school	2
9 Financial aid availability	4
10 Ability to fund for special needs	1

Step 2: The Design Step

The purpose in the design stage is two-fold: (1) to identify the appropriate funding vehicles for the college savings plan; and (2) to create a specific savings plan (i.e., monthly savings amount, expected return, etc).

Now that we understood Dean and Linda's savings goals and their plan benefits priority, we began to design their plan. Our first step was to identify the appropriate funding vehicle. In order to do this, we wanted to match the benefit priorities of the Scotts with the characteristics of the tools in our tool box. Figure 3.16 lists the major college planning tools and the benefits they add to a plan. The Scotts indicated the three most important benefits to design into their plan were:

1.   tax-free growth;

2.   tax-free distribution when used for qualified education expenses; and

3.   the custodian controls the distribution of funds.

The secondary factors were preservation of financial aid eligibility and investment control.

Based on the Scotts' benefits evaluation, two tools seemed to stand out as possibilities:

1.   529 college savings plans; and

2.   life insurance.

We noted that the Scotts already had adequate life insurance. In addition, the cost of life insurance would hold down their potential investment returns. Consequently, the funding tool of choice for the Scotts seemed to be the 529 college savings plan.

Figure 3.16
The College Planning Tools/Benefits Grid™

Tool	Tax Benefits		Financial Aid Friendly	Control		Estate Planning	Elementary/ Secondary School Use	Creditor Protection	Special Needs	Medical Plng
	Gr	Dist		Inv.	Dist.					
529 Plans										
Savings	Y	Y	Y	Y	Y	Y	N	Y	Y	Y
Prepaid	Y	Y	Y	N	Y	Y	N	Y	N	Y
Coverdell Education Savings Accounts	Y	Y	Y	Y	N	Y	N	Y	Y	N
UGMA/UTMA	N	N	N	Y	N	Y	Y	Y	Y	N
Life Insurance	Y	Y	Y	Y	Y	Y	Y	Y	Y	Y
Series EE & Series I Savings Bonds	Y	Y	N	Y	Y	N	N	N	N	Y
Roth IRA	Y	N	N	Y	Y	N	N	N	N	Y
Traditional IRA	Y	N	N	Y	Y	N	N	N	N	Y

The next step in this stage is to create a specific savings plan. We had already started this step in the discussion of lowering the target college costs to the state college level. When we had our plan design meeting with the Scotts, they had already begun to rethink their financial commitment to the college plan. They decided to definitively set their initial goal to fund for in-state college costs. The Scotts reaffirmed that they would begin their plan as soon as possible, commit to saving $500 per month ($6,000 annually) increasing by 5% per year, and transfer the lump sum of $10,000 they had already mentally committed into their plan. In addition, Linda informed us that she had talked to her parents about their Family Scholarship Plan and had been surprised when they volunteered to contribute $15,000. We reran the College Planning Conversation to show the Scotts their plan commitment and anticipated results. Those results are summarized in Figure 3.17.

Dean and Linda expressed surprise at the impact of Linda's parents' contribution to the Family Scholarship Plan. Figure 3.11 showed the Scotts initial plan. Figure 3.17 shows the final plan. The only difference was the contribution of $15,000 from Linda's parents. The table below summarizes the difference. Linda was excited to show this table to her parents to make them feel good about how much their contribution would help.

Plan Comparison C							
Plan Iteration	Total College Costs	Total Amount Saved	Total Loan Payments	Annual Loan Payments	Savings Period %	Spending & Borrowing Period %	Recovery Period %
Figure 3.11	$558,311	$211,007	$299,887	$37,486	24.0%	19.7%	56.3%
Figure 3.17	$558,311	$249,413	$205,225	$25,653	31.5%	23.2%	45.3%

Step 3: Plan Implementation

The steps in the plan implementation stage are as follows:

1. Choose the specific funding vehicle(s).

2. Set the asset allocation.

3. Choose the expectation benchmarks to measure performance.

4. Discuss the college/retirement link.

When helping the Scotts choose a specific funding vehicle for their college plan, we had them look at four separate factors:

1. advantages specific to their own state plan;

2. advisor-sold plans vs. direct-sold plans;

Figure 3.17

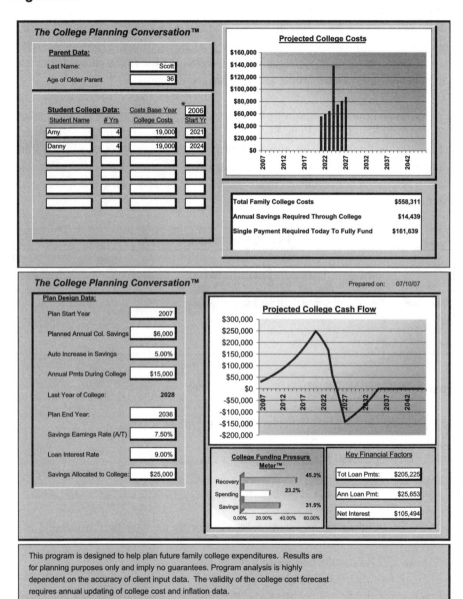

This program is designed to help plan future family college expenditures. Results are for planning purposes only and imply no guarantees. Program analysis is highly dependent on the accuracy of client input data. The validity of the college cost forecast requires annual updating of college cost and inflation data.

Version: 2007

*2006-2007

3.   fund family preferences; and

4.   performance and fees.

The Scotts live in New Jersey so that was the first state plan we analyzed. We determined that New Jersey does not provide a state income tax deduction. Consequently, there was not a tax advantage to using New Jersey's plan.

The second factor facing the Scotts was whether to use an advisor-sold plan or a direct-sold plan. A direct-sold plan would have lower fees because there are no commissions due to an advisor. The Scotts opted for the advisor-sold plan because they wanted the services an advisor can provide, including the annual monitoring that we will discuss in the next section. They opted for "C" share pricing over "A" share pricing. Although "A" share pricing would be cheaper in the long run, Dean and Linda wanted to be able to make changes in the plan if appropriate and they wanted their advisor to earn his compensation over time as he provided annual services.

Fund family selection and analysis of performance and fees are beyond the scope of this book. Two sources that provide substantial data on performance and fees are:

- www.morningstar.com

- www.savingforcollege.com

The next set of decisions facing the Scotts was setting the asset allocation. They opted for an age-based portfolio. Since the Scotts' children were very young, the plan would start with an aggressive portfolio and gradually become more conservative as the children get older. They indicated, however, that they expected their advisor to review the plan annually and suggest changes to the asset allocation, if appropriate.

We also engaged the Scotts in a discussion of performance expectations. Since they were investing in mutual funds, they needed to understand that performance could fluctuate dramatically and the returns could possibly go negative.

Satisfied with the structure of the plan, we added one final element to the Scotts' planning process—the college/retirement link. We explained that while we were dealing with college at this point, it was important not to ignore their retirement plan. Although retirement planning is not part of this book, it is important to make clients aware of the connection. We reminded the Scotts about the depth of the **recovery period** in their college plan and simply asked the following question:

Would you allow us to submit a proposal to you showing how we would help you manage your retirement funds in light of your college planning commitment?

The Scotts answered "yes" and we set up another appointment to begin their retirement planning.

Step 4: Monitor the Plan

To effectively monitor the plan, the advisor should:

1. arrange follow-up meetings to review performance;

2. meet at least annually;

3. review changes that may affect the plan; and

4. determine whether changes dictate a change in the plan.

Arranging a schedule for monitoring the plan may seem obvious, but this is an extremely important factor in the success of the plan. Many things can change, both within the family dynamic as well as externally, as a result of legislation and corporate decisions. One or more changes in the course of the year can have a huge impact on whether the plan will achieve its objectives.

In our office, performance monitoring is done on a quarterly basis and may or may not involve an actual meeting with the client. Plan performance is reviewed against selected benchmarks to make sure that underlying funds are at least keeping pace with the market as a whole.

On an annual basis, we provide families like the Scotts with the following services (at a minimum):

*   *An update of* the College Planning Conversation looking for: family changes; affirmation or changes of college planning goals; potential changes in contributions to the plan; and a review of plan performance by inserting actual plan values in the lump-sum section.

*   *An update of* the Financial Aid Test and the Financial Aid Appraisal. The closer the family gets to the start of college, the more accurate these tools will be. Should financial aid appear to be a significant factor, some restructuring of assets may be appropriate.

- *A reevaluation of* the benefit section of the Family Scholarship Plan to make sure that changes in the Scotts' requirements don't mandate changes in the plan.

At the same time, if anything has changed with respect to financial aid rules, tax legislation, or employer circumstances, etc., now is the time to evaluate the impact they might have on the plan.

Finally, the annual review is a good time to remind the Scotts of the impact that college will have on their ability to retire and to suggest a retirement plan review.

Eventually, the Scotts' children will enter high school. At that time they enter the Crisis Planning stage described in Chapter 4. Hopefully, if we have done our planning well, there won't be a major crisis. Many of the items described in the Crisis Planning case study that follows will become appropriate planning activities for the Scotts.

Chapter 4

CRISIS COLLEGE PLANS
FOR PARENTS

Whether or not a parent has saved for college, the planning process needs to change when the student enters high school. We call this the Crisis Planning stage. Although it is never too late to save, at this point the emphasis must be on other things. Since the college planning horizon is now fairly short, it is easier than before to predict whether cash flow from the need-based financial aid system will have a significant effect on the payment of college bills. The purpose of this stage is to decide whether or not the family will capitalize on need-based financial aid in their college financing plan, and then to adjust the rest of their planning accordingly.

There are three different planning scenarios in the Crisis Planning stage:

1. financial aid *will* be a significant factor;

2. financial aid *might* be significant depending on choices the student makes; or

3. financial aid likely *will not* be a significant factor.

Planning begins with the Financial Aid Test™ or an equivalent financial aid analysis. The family needs to input their financial data into the two financial aid formulas, the Federal Methodology and the Institutional Methodology, as though their student were going to begin college the next semester. The resulting Expected Family Contributions (EFC) will determine the appropriate planning category. The EFC is the amount of money that the financial aid system expects a family to contribute towards the cost of college based on the family's income and asset mix. For a more detailed description of how financial aid works, see Chapter 7.

Once the EFC is determined, it is time to choose a planning category. The following table shows how to define the planning categories.

How the Expected Family Contribution Determines the Crisis Planning Category	
Planning Category	**Expected Family Contribution Range**
Financial aid *will likely* be a significant factor	Under $20,000
Financial aid *might* be significant depending on choices the student makes	$20,000 – $50,000
Financial aid *likely will not* be a significant factor	Over $50,000

Why did we choose these seemingly arbitrary amounts shown in the table above? Since there are currently few colleges that cost over $50,000, a family expected to pay $50,000 or more will not receive any significant financial aid. Conversely, if the family EFC requires them to pay less than $20,000, they will receive significant aid for all but the least expensive schools. For those families expected to pay somewhere in between, it will depend on the cost of college in relation to the EFC as to whether or not financial aid will be a significant factor. Here is an example to bring this concept home:

The Miller family completes the Financial Aid Test (not shown) and has an EFC of $26,000. The EFC in this case happens to be the same under both the Federal Methodology and the Institutional Methodology. They are considering three different colleges for their daughter Mary. The table below shows why the Millers need to plan differently for each different choice.

Choosing a Planning Category			
	State College (in-state)	**Private College**	**Ivy League College**
Estimated Total Cost	$20,000	$35,000	$48,000
EFC	$26,000	$26,000	$26,000
Financial Need	- $6,000	$9,000	$22,000
Planning Category	Aid Unlikely	Aid Likely	Aid Likely

Although based on the first table above, Mary Miller initially falls in the middle planning category, she moves to one of the other planning categories as soon as she chooses a type of college. The middle planning category ("financial aid *might* be significant") is a temporary category. The potential for receiving aid becomes either "likely or "unlikely" as soon as the family makes its choices, which must be made before planning can be completed.

It may be helpful to use the Financial Aid Appraisal™ to get a financial aid projection before making a decision. The Financial Aid Appraisal will help the family visualize how significant the total amount of financial aid will be over the entire college period. Often the total family budget, or how significant the total amount of aid might be, influences these choices. Please note that this process is only a guide. Financial aid is college-specific, and only when the college releases a specific financial aid package will the student (in this case, Mary Miller) know exactly what he or she is getting. It is also important to note that the choice of college really should be based on the student's academic needs, first, and on financial aid considerations second.

Figure 4.1 is a flow chart of the process for a **Parent-Initiated Crisis Plan**. Although many of the planning steps appear to be the same across all of the categories, the focus should be different.

The easiest way to understand this process is to examine each planning track separately. Let's look at what needs to be done if we determine that financial aid is *likely* and we want to take advantage of the situation. Figure 4.2 isolates the "aid likely" track. As we can see there are a number of steps that we need to follow:

- *Determine the college budget.* In the case of a need-based financial aid candidate, the college budget is almost always equal to the EFC. Students will not be able to contribute much more since additional earned income on the part of the student will only increase the EFC. In addition, student loans will be part of the financial aid package and, therefore, not available to reduce the parents' cost. Students usually do not have much borrowing power beyond student loans because they generally do not have substantial income. A parent could co-sign other loans and later pass the burden on to the student if necessary.

- *Select appropriate colleges.* This is an important step. Students need to find colleges that meet as close to 100% of their need or there will be a financial aid gap that parents or students will need to make up, thus increasing the college budget. One good source to help manage this is: www.collegeboard.com/collegesearch. A great tool for tabulating the data is **the College Financial Aid History Comparison™** found in Chapter 8.

Figure 4.1 Parent-Initiated Crisis Planning

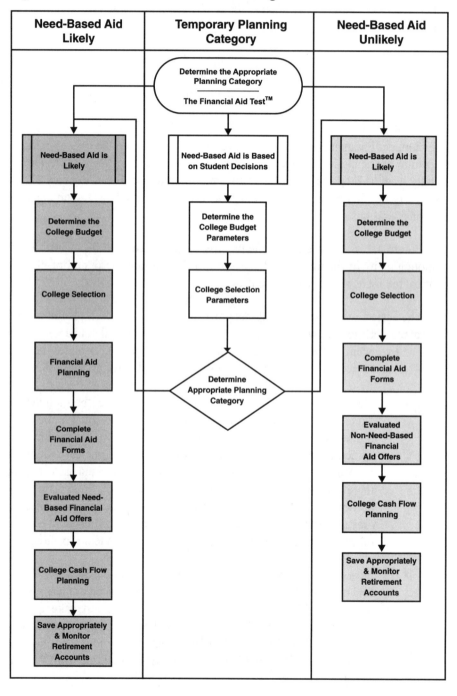

- *Evaluate financial aid planning options.* The purpose of financial aid planning is to ensure that additional parent or student income or assets don't jeopardize potential financial aid. The following examples can improve or minimize damage to potential financial aid:

  - UGMA accounts can be spent on legitimate expenses on behalf of the student in lieu of dollars a parent might have spent out-of-pocket on the same things.

  - Any savings should be put in the parents' names, not the student's.

  - Parents might pre-pay expenses (e.g., a mortgage payment) to reduce cash.

  The **Financial Aid Planning Checklist™** can offer some suggestions. In addition, advisors and parents can use **the Financial Aid Test** to check the effect of any suggested strategies.

- *Complete the appropriate financial aid forms on time.* Some schools require the FAFSA form, only, while others require both the FAFSA and the PROFILE form. Still other schools require the FAFSA, their own college form, and supplemental forms. The school will state which forms are required along with the appropriate deadlines. No matter which forms are required, a student's financial aid package will not get full attention until *all* forms are received. In addition, at some schools where financial aid dollars are tight, financial aid is awarded on a first come, first served basis. In other words, missing financial aid deadlines could cost the student money. Although one can file financial aid forms using estimates of income, all schools eventually require a copy of the most recent income tax returns for both parents and students. Forms and tax return data must agree before a final aid package will be awarded.

- *Evaluate need-based financial aid offers.* Once a financial aid package is awarded, a student should not automatically assume that it is correct. Need-based financial aid is reasonably predictable. An expected award can be calculated and compared to the actual award. If there is a significant difference, questions should be asked. Although there may be legitimate reasons for the difference, mistakes sometimes do happen, but they can be corrected. **The Financial Aid Package Evaluator™** is useful for evaluating the award from each school.

Figure 4.2 Parent-Initiated Crisis Planning
Need-Based Aid is Likely

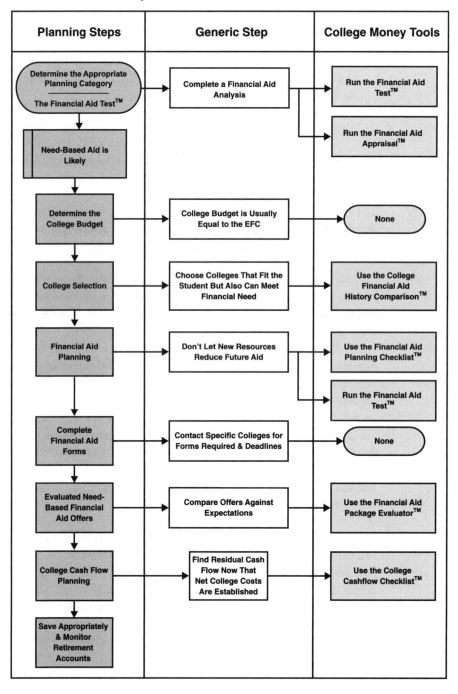

- *Cash flow planning.* Once the financial aid offer has been finalized, the family now knows exactly what they are expected to pay. Now they need to review possible sources of cash, including loans, and integrate the cash flow plan with their retirement plan. **The College Cash Flow Checklist™** can help locate sources of cash.

- *Continue to save appropriately and monitor retirement plans.* The sooner parents begin allocating cash from current income to college, the better. This often means that there is some cash buildup before the first college bill is received. Depositing this cash in the right place so that it does not negatively affect future financial aid is important. As a general rule, dollars should be kept in the parent's name and never in the student's name. The importance of monitoring retirement funds also should not be forgotten. Growth in existing retirement funds probably will be the major addition, and may in fact be the only addition to future retirement income, while parents focus on paying college bills.

Figure 4.3 shows the planning steps required when a student is *not likely* to qualify for need based financial aid:

- *Determine the college budget.* Unless a parent is willing to give a blank check to each of his or her children for college, the budgeting phase is critical. Parents often create extra stress in the college process by not giving their student financial guidelines at the beginning of the process. Students tend to choose colleges priced well beyond the family's ability to pay and then are disappointed when they are accepted and parents tell them they cannot go. Giving the student a budget at the outset can motivate the student to apply for special, non-need-based scholarships that might allow him to attend a more expensive college.

  Putting the budget together requires good financial planning technique. It is important to evaluate not only parent and student resources, but also to examine the commitment to educate other family members as well as the additional need to fund for retirement.

- *Select an appropriate college.* The most important part of this step is for the student to select colleges that meet his or her academic, athletic, and social needs. Once the family has identified these criteria, shopping for non-need-based scholarships and grants can significantly reduce the net cost of college. There are a large number of smaller private colleges that have realized they can attract high quality students by offering them non-need-based aid. The students these colleges seek are

Figure 4.3 Parent-Initiated Crisis Planning
Need-Based Financial Aid is Unlikely

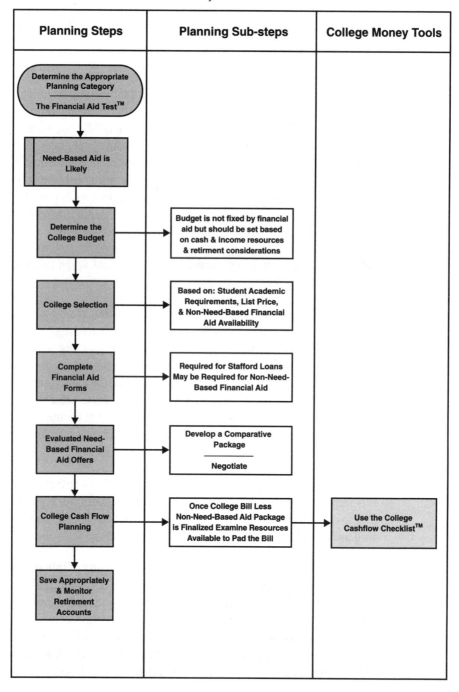

Planning Steps	Planning Sub-steps	College Money Tools
Determine the Appropriate Planning Category — The Financial Aid Test™		
Need-Based Aid is Likely		
Determine the College Budget	Budget is not fixed by financial aid but should be set based on cash & income resources & retirment considerations	
College Selection	Based on: Student Academic Requirements, List Price, & Non-Need-Based Financial Aid Availability	
Complete Financial Aid Forms	Required for Stafford Loans May be Required for Non-Need-Based Financial Aid	
Evaluated Need-Based Financial Aid Offers	Develop a Comparative Package — Negotiate	
College Cash Flow Planning	Once College Bill Less Non-Need-Based Aid Package is Finalized Examine Resources Available to Pad the Bill	Use the College Cashflow Checklist™
Save Appropriately & Monitor Retirement Accounts		

typically in the top 25% of the incoming freshman class. Unfortunately, there is no convenient list of these types of schools to review. Students can find out about the likelihood of receiving financial assistance by stating their credentials during a college interview and asking what special non-need-based scholarships are available for which they can apply. Since colleges are anxious to attract qualified students, this information will be gladly disseminated. When finalizing the list, it is important that either the list price of the college or the net cost (i.e., list price less non-need-based financial aid) be in the family's budget.

- *Complete financial aid forms.* Although a student in this planning category is not applying for traditional financial aid, filing some financial aid forms may be required to get unsubsidized student loans and non-need-based financial aid. Check with each college for requirements.

- *Evaluate non-need-based financial aid offers.* Sooner or later a desirable student will begin to receive non-need-based financial aid offers by mail. Some offers will be better than others. Should a student prefer to attend a college that has awarded a lower aid package than its competition, the student has two choices: (1) accept the lower package; or (2) try to negotiate for more money. Most colleges state that they will not negotiate—period! Nevertheless, experience has taught us colleges usually do not want to lose their preferred students. Instead of taking a negotiating stance, try the following steps:

  - Call the financial aid department of the college the student wishes to attend.

  - Inform them another college has offered a significantly more attractive aid package and before you accept that college's award, you would appreciate it if they would look at it to make sure you are not misunderstanding the package.

This softer approach may compel a college to increase its package. But students and parents should understand that each college has a preferred list of students. Whether or not they respond to such an request is dependent on how high on the preferred list the student is.

- *Plan college cash flow.* Once the final aid package has been determined, it is time to calculate the final college cost. Parents need to finalize their college cash flow plan. **The College Cash Flow Planning Checklist** can be useful in finding sources of funds.

- *Continue to save and monitor retirement resources.* The sooner parents begin allocating cash from current income to college, the better. This often means that there is some cash buildup before the parents receive the first college bill. Unlike the "likely aid" category, parents in this situation do not need to worry about the effect of cash build up on future financial aid. Rather, standard convenience and tax issues should determine planning considerations. And do not forget the importance of monitoring retirement funds. Growth in existing retirement funds will probably still be the major addition, and perhaps the only addition to future retirement income, while parents focus on paying college bills.

THE DILLON FAMILY: CRISIS COLLEGE PLANNING

Step 1: Diagnostics

Jack and Nina Dillon are both 47 years old. They have a daughter, Melissa, who is in her junior year of high school. They have accumulated only $32,000 in their college account and recognize they do not have nearly enough saved to pay their anticipated college bills. With two younger children to educate as well, they are very concerned about how they will handle the college years and want to get a head start on the process. The Dillon family attended a workshop, and came into the office for the results of their Financial Aid Test.

When we presented the Dillons with their test results, we informed them of both the good news and the bad. The bad news is: if they send their children to state colleges as in-state residents, most likely they will *not* qualify for financial aid. Since their Federal Family Expected Contribution (FEC) of $30,479 is greater than $19,000 (the cost of a state school in New Jersey, Rutgers), they would be expected to pay the full cost.

The good news is that most likely the Dillons most likely *would qualify* for aid at higher priced private colleges. Many of the private colleges use the Institutional Methodology as their dominant financial aid tool. The Dillon's Family Expected Contribution (FEC) under the Institutional Methodology is $25,825, actually less than their Federal Methodology EFC (note: we use the terms EFC and FEC interchangeably).

If Melissa attends a private college that uses the Institutional Methodology, the Dillons will be expected to pay $25,825, and if they choose colleges with enough funds to make up the difference, the rest would be paid by the financial aid system. The table on the next page summarizes Melissa's financial aid status.

Choosing a Planning Category			
	State College (In-State) (Low)	Private College (Medium)	Ivy League College (High)
Total Cost	$19,000	$29,182	$43,341
FEC Federal Methodology	$30,479	N/A	N/A
FEC Institutional Methodology	N/A	$25,825	$25,825
Financial Need	- $11,479	$3,357	$17,516
Eligible	No	Yes	Yes

We reiterated to the Dillons that financial aid is not all free money—some of these dollars might be awarded in the form of student loans or work-study jobs. However, from a cash flow perspective, their college bills will be handled.

The dilemma for the Dillon family is whether they should push Melissa to the less expensive state colleges and cap their college budget at about $20,000 plus college inflation for the next four years, or capture the opportunity to send their children to higher priced private or even Ivy League colleges at a substantial discount? To make this decision, they need to look at two things: (1) the needs of each of their three children; and (2) the financial obligations under each scenario.

The Dillons have three children. Melissa (age 16) will start college in September of 2008. She is an "A" student, captain of the high school swim team, and has high PSAT scores. She has expressed interest in going to Yale in a pre-law program. Brian (age 13) will start college in 2011. He is less outgoing than his sister is and tends to do better in smaller classes where he gets more individual attention. Although it is too early to be sure, the Dillons think that a smaller private college would probably be most appropriate for him. Ben (age 9) will start college in 2015. At this time, the Dillons have no idea of what type of college would be appropriate for him. But in order to be fair, they want to plan for a private college for Ben, too.

To help the Dillons with this financial decision, we ran the Financial Aid Appraisal™ (Figure 4.5) showing their respective college preferences (i.e., Ivy League for Melissa, private colleges for Brian and Ben) and using their **Institutional Methodology Parent Expected Contribution (PEC)**.

Figure 4.4

The Financial Aid Test™

Version 2007
01-Aug-07

Family Data:

Parent's Name (in report form)	Dillon
Student's Name (in report form)	Melissa
Street Address	9876 Main Street
City, State, ZIP	Passaic, NY 01234
Home Telephone:	856-000-0000
Business Telephone:	856-000-0000
State of Residence (All Caps, eg. NJ)	NJ
1 Age of Older Parent	47
2 Number of Parents in Family	2
3 Number of Dependent Children in Family	3
4 Number of Students in College for Plan Year	1
5 Total Ages of All Pre-college Children	22

Student Financial Data:

23 Student's Assets	$0
24 Student's Income	
a From Work	$4,000
b From Investments	$0
25 Student Income Tax Paid	$0
26 Assets in Siblings Names (IM only)	$0

Parent Financial Data:

6	Father's Wages	$101,000
7	Mother's Wages	$42,000
8	Other Taxable Income	$780
9	Nontaxable income	$0
10	Untaxed Benefits	$0
11	Losses from Business, Farm, Capital Los	$0
12	Adjustments to Income	$0
13	Child Support Paid	$0
14	Tuition Tax Credits	$0
15	Taxable Student Aid	$0
16	Medical & Dental Expense	$5,000
17	Federal Income Taxes Paid	$17,000
18	Net Home Equity (include farm if you live on it)	
	a Market Value	$358,000
	b Sum of All Mortgages	$253,000
19	Net Equity of Other Real Estate	
	a Market Value	$0
	b Sum of All Mortgages	$0
20	Business/Farm Net Value (Your Share)	
	a Business Net Value	$0
	b Farm Net Value (if not used as residenc	$0
21	Parent Cash	$5,000
22	Parent Investments	
	a Qualified Retirement Plans	$475,000
	b Other	$32,000
	Debts other than mortgages	$0

The Financial Aid Test™ - Quick Calc

Federal Methodology

Parent Expected Cont./Student	$30,212
Student Expected Contribution	$267
Expected Family Contribution/Student	$30,479

Key Counseling Numbers — Federal Methodology

	Assets	Income
% EPC From:	0.00%	100.00%
% ESC From:	0.00%	100.00%
Par. Marg.Cont.:	5.64%	47.00%
Stud. Marg. Cont:	20.00%	50.00%

Institutional Methodology

Parent Expected Cont./Student	$23,988
Student Expected Contribution	$1,837
Expected Family Contribution/Student	$25,825

Key Counseling Numbers — Institutional Methodology

	Assets	Income
% EPC From:	5.79%	94.21%
% ESC From:	0.00%	100.00%
Par. Marg. Cont:	4.00%	46.00%
Stud. Marg. Cont:	25.00%	50.00%

This analysis provides estimated financial aid data for planning purposes only. Actual financial aid awards are determined by each college at the time of admission. The validity of the input data can dramatically affect financial aid values. Which assets must be counted and how each asset is valued may be treated differently by the government and each individual college. Calculations are based on:
Federal Methodology   2007-08

Institutional Methodology   2007-08

Source: "CSS/Financial Aid PROFILE® User's Guide"

Copyright © 2007-08 The College Board, www.collegeboard.com.

Reproduced with permission.

The Institutional Methodology Worksheet and Computational Tables may be used by the individual purchaser of the CD but may not be posted on any website or reproduced in any other digital format without the express written consent of the College Board.

Figure 4.5

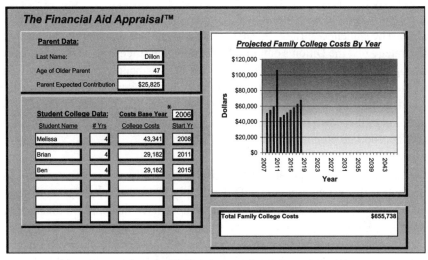

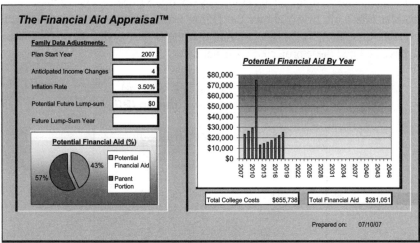

This program is designed to help families plan for future college expenditures. It projects future college costs and future financial aid eligibility based on current and past college cost data and current financial aid formulas which can change substantially over time. **This program is intended for planning purposes only and implies no guarantees.**

Projecting college costs and financial aid can be useful in the planning process to help decide on savings commitments and college funding vehicles. But for best results, projections should be recalculated annually using the most current version of this spreadsheet.

Version: 2007

*2006-2007

Note that we are using the *Parent* Expected Contribution instead of the *Family* Expected Contribution. The Family Expected Contribution (FEC) is equal to the Parent Expected Contribution (PEC) plus the Student Expected Contribution (SEC). The student contribution can vary substantially depending on the financial aid strategy that the Dillon's employ. The amount the student earns the year before starting college and the manner in which the Dillons handle any student savings can make a difference. If they opt to maximize financial aid, the Dillons can, and should, control these factors. It is less likely, however, that they will have realistic control over their own income and assets. Thus the Parent Expected Contribution is the appropriate number to use.

Figure 4.5, the Financial Aid Appraisal, graphically summarizes most of the information that is important to the Dillon family. Their projected total college bill will be $655,738 based on the choices the Dillons have made. If the financial aid projections hold true, (i.e., there are no significant changes in their income, assets, or the financial aid rules and formulas), and the Dillons choose colleges able to meet their financial need, financial aid could pay up to $281,051 or 43% of their college bill. The first table below shows the Dillon family's Projected Parent Expected Contribution (PEC). This is the amount that the Dillons will be expected to pay. We have isolated these projected costs below.

The Dillon Family's Projected Parent Expected Contribution (PEC)	
Institutional Methodology	
Year	**PEC**
2008	$27,000
2009	$28,229
2010	$29,513
2011	$30,856
2012	$32,260
2013	$33,728
2014	$35,262
2015	$36,867
2016	$38,544
2017	$40,298
2018	$42,131
Total	$374,687

Dillon's Preliminary College Cash Flow	
The Dillions will need	$374,687
The Dillions currently have	$32,000
Balance required	$342,687
Working years to retirement	18
Annualized commitment to college (now until retirement)	$28,557

Thus, on a preliminary cash flow basis, the Dillons would need to come up with approximately $28,557 each year beginning in 2007 through 2025 when they retire.

We brought out the college planning flowchart (Figure 4.6) and showed the Dillons the planning steps that apply to their situation. Initially, they were in the middle category; but because of the choices they made regarding higher priced colleges, they need to plan as a **Likely Financial Aid Candidate.**

DETERMINE THE COLLEGE BUDGET

The Dillons' college budget has largely been determined for them. It is their Parent Expected Contribution. Their children will not be able to help much since any savings or income they might add would simply increase the total family expected contribution and, therefore, reduce total financial aid. In addition, student loans will most likely be part of the financial aid package and, thus, will not help with the parent portion of the college costs. There may be other loans their children can apply for, but they are limited since students have virtually no income or assets not earmarked for direct college costs. The cash flow outlined in the Dillon Family's Projected Parent Expected Contribution (PEC) table is generally what the Dillon Family will need to deal with.

College Selection

College selection will be critical for the Dillon's children. They need to look for colleges that can meet as close to 100% of their need as possible. The Dillon family will need to make up any difference to the extent that colleges meet less than 100% of their financial need.

The first step in the college selection process is for Melissa to generate a list of colleges that are appropriate to her academic and social needs. Once she has

Figure 4.6 Flowchart

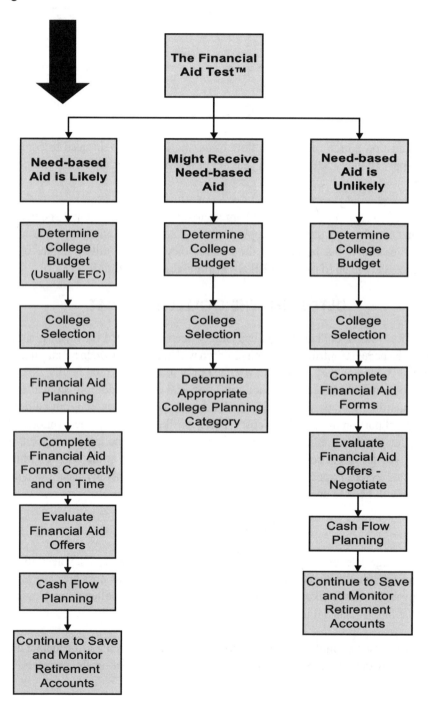

carefully researched the schools on the list, the Dillon family will need to look at the affordability of each school while also keeping in mind the appropriateness of each school for Melissa. It is important to remember that the family will be paying at least a part of the bill, and they will not get the value they wish if a school cannot meet the needs of Melissa. The availability of free money—even if the amount of aid to be awarded is substantial—has to be secondary to the suitability of the school for the student.

Melissa spent a great deal of time talking to parents, teachers, guidance counselors, and friends about what she wanted out of a college. In addition, she used school and library resources to develop her list. She looked at what major courses of study were available, the academic difficulty and competitiveness of each school, campus and social life, and other factors she thought might be important. Figure 4.7 contains the schools Melissa felt were appropriate for her academic and social needs. Note that the financial aid information in the table is merely a hypothetical approximation of various college financial aid packages (i.e., the figures do not represent actual financial aid information for any college).

Figure 4.7

The College Financial Aid History Comparison™					
School Name	**Average Financial Aid Package ($)**	**% of Need Met**	**% of Aid in Grants**	**% of Aid in Loans or Jobs**	**Forms Required**
Ivy League College 1	$27,500	100%	85%	15%	FAFSA PROFILE
Ivy League College 2	$31,500	100%	89%	11%	FAFSA PROFILE
High-Priced Private College 1	$28,000	100%	Not Reported	Not Reported	FAFSA PROFILE
High-Priced Private College 2	$28,000	100%	83%	17%	FAFSA PROFILE
High-Priced Private College 3	$28,000	98%	77%	23%	FAFSA PROFILE
State University	$11,500	69%	44%	56%	FAFSA (only)

Most of the colleges on Melissa's list meet 100% of need. This means that if the Dillon family can come up with their Parent Expected Contribution (PEC) and Melissa can come up with her Student Expected Contribution (SEC), the rest of the cash flow required to pay college bills should be taken care of. High Priced

College 3 is an exception, although not a major one. Since High Priced Private College 3 will meet only 98% of the Dillon's financial need, the family will need to make up the difference. State University does not come close to providing enough financial aid, but the Dillons will not qualify for financial aid at State University anyway, so it is a moot point. If Melissa chooses to attend State University, the Dillons will pay the full cost, but a cost that is less than the net cost they would pay after financial aid at the other schools.

PLAN TO ENHANCE THE FINANCIAL AID PACKAGE

There are some financial advisors who attempt to hide parent and student assets in order to "package" students to get more financial aid. Most of the time these ploys not only border on being unethical, but they are also complicated—and, often, they simply do not work. College financial aid people are smart. They ask questions designed to spot hidden assets. They have even prosecuted parents and financial advisors, requesting as much as triple damages and jail time when parents have not properly disclosed assets and personal data. There are some things, however, that not only are legitimate, but also make sense to employ. We partially summarize these strategies in the Financial Aid Planning Checklist™ (Figure 4.8).

First, the Dillons needed to start saving money before college as part of their preliminary cash flow plan. It is important that they save this money in their own names, as opposed to their children's names, because dollars saved in parent-owned accounts reduce financial aid awards by about 6% whereas dollars saved in student-owned accounts reduce financial aid awards by 20% or more. (See the financial aid rules in Chapter 7).

Because Melissa plans to work and save money for college, we suggested that the Dillons set up a joint savings account using one parent's Social Security number to hold those funds. Melissa will still have access to the joint account. But using the Social Security number of one of her parents also means that the account will be considered a parent account for financial aid purposes. The parents will be responsible for taxes, but we anticipate those to be minimal.

We also investigated other options that turned out to be inappropriate in this case:

- Had the Dillons needed a new car, we would have suggested using parent cash to purchase it. A small amount of parent cash would have decreased family assets for financial aid purposes, and cars do not count as assets.

Figure 4.8

Financial Aid Planning Checklist™
Remember that students must apply for financial aid *each* year. If the student is a marginal financial aid candidate, families might be able to "create" financial aid eligibility by using some of the strategies below to target certain years (e.g., those years when there would be two students in college at the same time). This is a suggested list, and should not be considered complete.

Reduce Student Assets:	✓ Use funds in UGMA/UTMA accounts for nonparental student expenses. ✓ Re-title non-UGMA/UTMA accounts in joint names with a parent's Social Security number.
Control Student Income	✓ Federal Methodology will not include up to the first $3,000 of student income. ✓ Institutional Methodology will impute $1,550 of student income, whether it is earned or not.
Control Parent Income	✓ Difficult for W-2 earnings, but possible if a parent can control when they receive bonuses, commissions, etc. ✓ Consider carefully that a nonworking spouse returning to work might reduce financial aid by increasing parent income. ✓ Liquidation of investments may generate taxable income that can negatively affect the following year's financial aid award.
Reduce Parent Assets	✓ Increase mortgage payments—this will not necessarily affect treatment of home equity as an asset, but can reduce cash assets. ✓ Use caution when considering repositioning of assets to hide them from financial aid officers. This is a risky strategy that may not work, and may tie-up assets and render them unusable for college in later years.
Divorced/ Separated Parents	✓ Have the lower-income parent become the custodial parent and apply for financial aid. ✓ This strategy may not work for schools using the Institutional Methodology, because they will ask for the income and assets of the noncustodial parent and stepparent as well.

- Prepaying mortgage payments can also reduce parent cash. Since they are mostly interest anyway, they do not increase home equity by a like amount.

- Spending the soon-to-be college student's UGMA money on appropriate expenses on behalf of the student can also improve financial aid awards.

COMPLETE FINANCIAL AID FORMS

Since the Dillon family is depending on financial aid, it is critical that they complete all required forms *on time*. They will also have to complete their income taxes early, if possible, because colleges will eventually require copies of tax returns to be submitted in order to verify financial aid form information. Although families can file forms with estimated tax data, an aid award will not be official, and could even be amended, after final tax forms are received.

Each college has its own form requirements. Some colleges want only the Free Application for Federal Student Aid (FAFSA), while others want the FAFSA *and* the PROFILE. And some colleges require college specific forms and supplements to the PROFILE. The only way to know for sure what is needed is to contact the college and ask for that school's requirements and due dates in writing. Due dates can be critical! Colleges usually process only completed packages. Candidates for financial aid with incomplete packages may get less if funds become tight.

EVALUATE FINANCIAL AID OFFERS

Usually colleges do not offer final financial aid packages until spring of the senior year. The exception is an early admissions candidate who may receive an offer earlier in the year. Once the acceptance letters are in, and any financial aid offers arrive, Jack and Nina will only have a few weeks to evaluate the offers. In the case of a need-based financial aid candidate, evaluating offers is fairly straightforward. The purpose of the evaluation is to make sure that no mistakes were made, as explained below:

1. Rerun the Financial Aid Test using the actual numbers that were used on the official financial aid forms. The results should be accurate.

2. Obtain the total cost of college from the college budget bill.

3. Extract from the Financial Aid Test the appropriate Family Expected Contribution (FEC). For example, if the college requires the PRO-

FILE form, use the Institutional Methodology FEC; otherwise use the Federal FEC. Note that the college will base its financial aid award on the Family Expected Contribution (FEC), not the Parent Expected Contribution (PEC).

4. Calculate financial need (Step 2 minus Step 3).

5. Determine the percentage of need met for this college. Multiply the percentage of need met times financial need as calculated in Step 4. This should approximate the total amount of aid awarded by the college.

6. Determine the percentage in the form of grants number. Multiply the percentage by financial need as calculated in Step 4. This should approximate the total grants awarded by the college.

7. Identify the percentage of aid in loans and jobs for this college. Multiply the percentage by financial need calculated in Step 4. This should approximate the percentage of loans and jobs awarded by the college.

Use Figure 4.9 for each school at which the student has been accepted.

If the actual aid package differs from the results calculated in Figure 4.10, the Dillons should call the financial aid office at the college and ask questions. Sometimes mistakes happen. That is the major reason why parents should validate financial aid awards.

On the other hand, there may be a valid reason why a college does not meet a family's expected aid package. Parents and students may get less than expected under the followings circumstances:

•   *Strength of student* – if financial aid is scarce, colleges will sometimes reward those students that they really want, and give lesser awards to marginal applicants.

•   *Change of policy* – for example, a college diverts some of their need-based funds to merit awards.

•   *Adverse financial circumstances* – a college could suffer a financial decline in their endowment and could decide to parcel aid awards differently than in past years.

In Figure 4.10 we completed a hypothetical result so that the Dillons could see how the analysis might work.

Figure 4.9

The Financial Aid Package Evaluator™ College Name: _____		
1. Actual College Costs (from the college)		
2. Family Expected Contribution (Note: Use updated Financial Aid Test™ results. If college uses PROFILE, use Institutional Methodology; otherwise, use federal methodology. Run using numbers from the actual PROFILE or FAFSA input data.)		
3. % Need Met (from the college financial aid package)		
4. Expected Financial Need $((1 - 2) \times 3)$		
5. Actual Total Financial Aid Package (from the college)		
6. % Grants (from the College Board website)		
7. Expected Grants (4×6)		
8. Actual Grants (from the college financial aid package)		
9. % Loans & Jobs (from the College Board website)		
10. Expected Loans & Jobs (4×9)		
11. Actual Loans & Jobs (from the college financial aid package)		

Figure 4.10

The Financial Aid Package Evaluator™ College Name: Hypothetical Private College			
1. Actual College Costs (from the college)			$48,500
2. Family Expected Contribution (Note: Use updated Financial Aid Test™ results. If college uses PROFILE, use Institutional Methodology; otherwise, use federal methodology. Run using numbers from the actual PROFILE or FAFSA input data.)		$23,000	
3. % Need Met (from the college financial aid package)	90%		
4. Expected Financial Need ((1 − 2) x 3)		$17,212	
5. Actual Total Financial Aid Package (from the college)			$20,000
6. % Grants (from the College Board website)	75%		
7. Expected Grants (4 x 6)		$17,212	
8. Actual Grants (from the college financial aid package)			$17,500
9. % Loans & Jobs (from the College Board website)	25%		
10. Expected Loans & Jobs (4 x 9)		$5,738	
11. Actual Loans & Jobs (from the college financial aid package)			$2,500

In this hypothetical example, the Dillons actually received a smaller financial aid package than they expected; however, they also received a larger grant than expected. The Dillons probably should call the college and ask about the smaller than expected package.

CASH FLOW PLANNING

In Figure 4.10, we assigned the Dillon family a preliminary cash flow figure. Now that exact college costs have been determined, we will be able to produce a more accurate spreadsheet. Our experience is that most of the cash flow process discussed here is not unique to college planning and, in fact, it varies so widely that an example here would not be helpful. What advisors really need to put into the cash flow planning picture into perspective are the typical sources of cash to pay college costs from Figure 4.11.

There are also some unique tax savings tools with which advisors need to be familiar. These include the Hope Scholarship Credit and the Lifetime Learning Credit (discussed in detail in Chapter 7). There are also some unique loans (also discussed in Chapter 7) that should be investigated before an advisor settles on a home equity arrangement.

It is particularly important that families like the Dillons not deplete their cash reserves. College can extend over a lengthy period of time and cash reserves might be required to help the family pay unexpected expenses that arise in the future.

It is also important that the Dillons not raid their retirement funds to pay for college. It's easy to borrow from a 401(k) plan, but the withdrawal takes away dollars that will be needed later for retirement. Parents also don't realize that these dollars are growing tax-free. When retirement dollars are withdrawn or borrowed, parents lose this big advantage. Finally, we often see parents getting hit with unexpected tax bills from a retirement plan withdrawal or a loan that inadvertently triggered a premature distribution.

CONTINUE TO SAVE AND MONITOR
RETIREMENT ACCOUNTS

The Dillon family should monitor their financial aid eligibility by completing a Financial Aid Test at least annually. Changes in their financial aid status could drastically affect how they plan for their younger children.

The Dillons also need to continue to save as much as possible. Savings should be titled in their own names (not the student's) or directed into their retirement qualified plans in order to preserve as much financial aid eligibility as possible.

A major potential problem for the Dillon family is retirement. Although retirement planning is not part of this book, the manner in which we open a retirement

Figure 4.11

	College Cash Flow Planning Checklist™
✓	This is not necessarily a complete list
	Financial Aid Package (from college financial aid office) Pell Grant SEOG Grant Perkins Loan Subsidized Stafford Loan Work/Study College/University scholarship/grant College/University loan
	Other Scholarships State scholarships/grants Private scholarships (VFW, etc.) Employer scholarships
	Savings Parents' Students'
	Current Income Parents' Students'
	Tax Savings Hope Scholarship Credit Lifetime Learning Credit Student loan interest deduction
	Contributions from Relatives Direct tuition payments Gifts (after financial aid award received)
	Student Loans (not part of the financial aid package) Unsubsidized Stafford Loans Signature loans State loans
	Parent Loans Mortgage refinance (cash out) Home equity loan Home equity line of credit PLUS loan Private loans
	Life Insurance Loans
	Retirement Accounts Traditional IRA Roth IRA 401(k)
	Use careful consideration before using retirement accounts to pay for college. Taxes may be due, premature distributions may result, or future retirement income can be adversely affected. Consult a financial advisor.

case from a college planning case is a major part. We found that the following series of simple statements and questions convinced the Dillons to let us handle their retirement accounts.

The College/Retirement Link

Our research has shown that there are only four ways to have more money in your retirement account:

- First, you can save more. With your current commitment to college, how much more can you put aside for retirement?

- Second, your employer can put more aside for you. How likely is this over the next several years?

- Third, you can inherit money, or win the lottery. How likely is this for you?

- Fourth, you can do a better job of managing your existing retirement plan, attempting to improve returns, and controlling risk. We do this for many parents of college students. Would you allow us to submit a proposal to you on how we would do this for you?

Interestingly, we have never received a "no" in response to our request to submit a proposal for handling retirement from a crisis college planning parent. Although we don't always get the retirement accounts, college planning parents are concerned and they will give you all of the information you need to do the retirement analysis. Sometimes all of the retirement money is tied up in a 401(k) plan and can't be moved currently. We offer to review the retirement plan asset allocation on an annual basis for the client and help the client rebalance plan assets, if needed. We usually charge a small fee for this service. If you keep in touch, when the client changes jobs or retires, these funds ultimately become available to you as the advisor of choice. We currently have an inventory of millions of dollars currently unavailable to us because they are in 401(k) plans. Our experience indicates, however, that at the appropriate time we'll get our share of these funds, simply because we have kept in touch and established a professional relationship.

Chapter 5

GRANDPARENT COLLEGE PLANS

Grandparents can make a significant contribution to college planning. Historically, with many wealthier families it was traditionally the responsibility of the grandparents to pay for college. In subsequent years, however, this practice did not hold true for middle-income families. But recent soaring college costs have made it much more likely that, going into the future, grandparents may once again influence the planning for, and payment of, the high costs of college.

There are two major differences in planning structures and they relate to time horizons. Planning needs are different for students in high school than for those who are in lower grades. For high school students, grandparents should focus on the **Grandparent-Initiated Crisis Savings Plan** strategies, whereas for younger students they should focus on the **Grandparent-Initiated Long-Term Savings Plan** process.

GRANDPARENT-INITIATED LONG-TERM SAVINGS PLANS

Figure 5.1 shows an overview of the process for developing **Grandparent-Initiated Long-term Savings Plans**. Please note that the process is similar to developing **Parent-Initiated Plans** except:

- There is some additional data gathering to be done in the **Diagnostic Step**. **The Family Scholarship Plan™** conversation needs to be held not once but twice: once with the grandparent, and once with the parent.

- The emphasis on retirement planning in the **Monitoring Step** is different. Since the grandparent is volunteering college funds, as opposed to the parent who may be required to provide college funds, there isn't the same pressure. Hopefully, the grandparent is not jeopardizing his retirement to help his grandchildren as parents often do for their own children. There is, however, an opportunity to assist the grandparent with managing his financial resources that can be earned by creating a successful college plan and, consequently, a happy grandparent client.

Figure 5.1 Grandparent-Initiated Long-Term Savings Plans
Overview

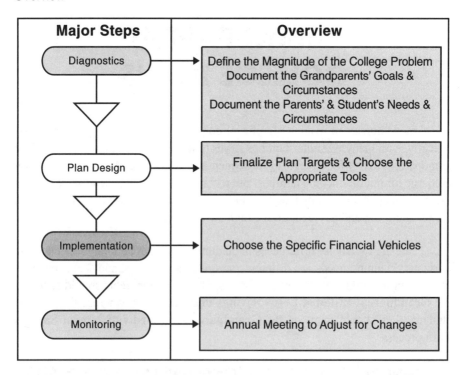

Major Steps	Overview
Diagnostics	Define the Magnitude of the College Problem Document the Grandparents' Goals & Circumstances Document the Parents' & Student's Needs & Circumstances
Plan Design	Finalize Plan Targets & Choose the Appropriate Tools
Implementation	Choose the Specific Financial Vehicles
Monitoring	Annual Meeting to Adjust for Changes

Since the major changes occur in the **Diagnostic Step**, we've included Figure 5.2 showing the sub-steps and the College Money tools that are available to help you. We are not going to review the other major steps here because of their similarity to the steps in the **Parent-Initiated Long-Term Savings Plans**.

The **Diagnostic Step** is broken down into three parts:

1. Grandparent Diagnostics;

2. Parent Diagnostics; and

3. Composite Diagnostics.

The first goal of the **Grandparent Diagnostics** is to document the magnitude of the college problem so that the grandparents can decide the level of commitment to college funding they wish to make. Although many grandparents start with a planned financial commitment already in mind, they may be motivated to do even more if they understand the entire problem. In addition, by taking the time to de-

Figure 5.2 Grandparent-Initiated Long-term Savings Plans
Diagnostics

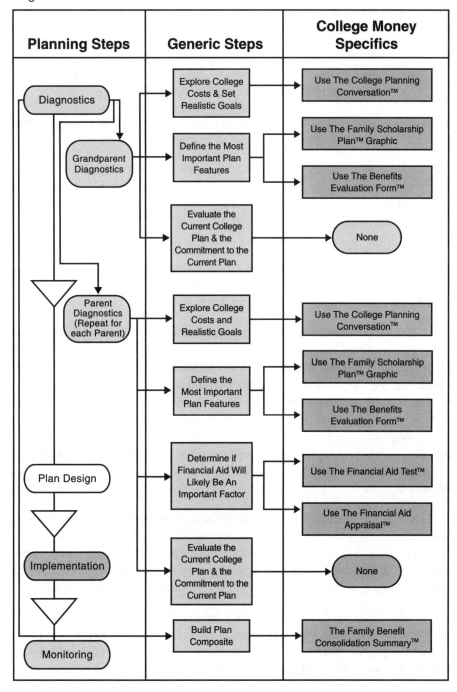

fine the problem, grandparents will better understand the magnitude of the college problem and reap more satisfaction from the contribution they are making. **The College Planning Conversation™** is an ideal way to help grandparents do this. As a financial advisor, you may wish to have this conversation from two different points of view:

- First, lump all grandchildren together in one analysis. This will show the entire cost of college for all of the grandchildren.

- Second, separate out each family. This will demonstrate the impact of college costs on each set of parents' ability to retire.

The second goal is to help the grandparents define the benefits of the college plan from their own perspective. This is best done by having a **Family Scholarship Plan** conversation and recording the grandparents' priorities on the **Benefits Evaluation Form™**. This will begin to create the financial specifications for the college plan.

If the grandparent has an existing plan of some kind, make sure you understand not only the resources that might be transferable from the old plan to the new plan, but also understand what worked well in the old plan and what didn't work so well. This data will be extremely helpful in final plan design.

Next, get the grandparents to set up meetings for you to talk with the parents of the grandchildren. The grandparents should inform each set of parents that they are setting up a **Family Scholarship Plan** for their grandchildren. They want to ensure that their deposits to the plan are focused for maximum benefits, and they need their children's help in going this. The grandparents are especially concerned that the plan does not hurt their grandchildren's ability to qualify for future potential financial aid. The grandparents should assure their children that any financial data the parents give to the grandparent's planner will be kept confidential from the grandparent, and that the grandparent will get only summary results for plan design purposes.

Each parent meeting should consist of the **College Planning Conversation** to discover parental goals and quantify any existing plans. This discussion also sets the stage for a potential new client relationship with the parent. You will have the opportunity to meet with each parent later to show them how the grandparent contribution will benefit each of their children and what is left for them, as parents, to do.

In addition to the **College Planning Conversation**, each parent needs to have the **Family Scholarship Plan** conversation and complete the **Benefits Evaluation Form** from their perspective. Of paramount importance is completing the **Financial Aid Test™** and a **Financial Aid Appraisal™** as part of the process. Financial aid consideration is often the wildcard that makes a grandparent plan successful, or not. Not only is this a critical piece of data for plan design, but it will also gives the advisor financial insight into whether or not to pursue a client relationship with the parent in the future. **The Financial Aid Test** is a great device to help you qualify potential prospects because the process will disclose the parents' complete income and asset picture to you.

After the initial meetings with the grandparents and each of the parents are complete, you can prepare the **Family Benefits Consolidation Summary™**. You may wish to prepare one of these forms for each student. Figure 5.3 shows a sample **Family Benefits Consolidation Summary**. This chart is similar to the **Benefits Evaluation Form**, but it has an extra column so that student needs and benefits are listed side-by-side with grandparent needs and benefits. There are also two rows near the top of the form: one to identify the student and show his age, and the other for identifying the planning horizon for that student (i.e., long-term saving or crisis).

Now you have all the data to return to the grandparent and begin the **Design Step**. The Design Step in a Grandparent-Initiated Plan is similar to the Design Step in a Parent-Initiated Plan.

Figure 5.3

Family Benefit Consolidation Summary™		
	Grandparent Data	**Student Data**
Name(s)/Age(s)		
Planning Status (Long-Term/Crisis)		
Tax-free growth		
Tax-free distributions		
Investment control		
Distribution control		
Estate planning		
Creditor protection		
Medical planning		
Ability to pay for private elementary and secondary school		
Financial aid availability		
Ability to fund for special needs		

GRANDPARENT-INITIATED CRISIS COLLEGE PLANNING

At the crisis level, planning becomes fairly simple. There is not a lot of time to save or invest, so the problem is one of transferring dollars to the student in a way that will benefit both the student and the grandparent. If the grandparent can't or won't fund the full college bill, then the grandparent should be sensitive to the grandchild's eligibility for financial aid.

It is important to discuss the **Family Scholarship Plan™** to uncover the benefits that the grandparent will appreciate most, and then have the same **Family Scholarship Plan** discussion with the parent. In both cases, the **Benefits Evaluation Form** should be completed. Special attention must be paid to potential financial aid, and the **Financial Aid Test** should be run. After all parents and the grandparents have been interviewed, the **Family Benefits Consolidation Summary** should be compiled.

Because this a crisis situation with a shorter planning time horizon, many of the benefits listed in the **Family Scholarship Plan** will be less relevant than usual, while others will be more significant. For example:

- Income taxes will be less important because there won't be interest and growth accumulations to deal with, simply because time horizons are shorter.

- Some states offer significant state income tax deductions for contributions to a 529 plan.

- Tax considerations could still be important if appreciated property is transferred as part of a college plan.

- Gift taxes might still be significant.

- Financial aid is often a dominant factor, so the Financial Aid Test is critical.

Usually, in a crisis plan, the main difference in planning strategy is usually the financial aid eligibility of the student. Here are some possibilities that a grandparent might consider, given two different planning scenarios:

Scenario 1: Grandchild is **eligible for need-based financial aid**:

- Wait until financial aid is awarded each year. Give dollars to the parent or student and instruct them to pay the dollars immediately towards the college bill.

- Give spending money directly to the student (Pizza Money Plan)

- Hold funds until after college. Give dollars to student to pay back student loans, or give dollars to parents to pay off college debt.

Scenario 2: Grandchild is **not eligible for need-based financial aid eligible**:

- Make payment directly to the college on behalf of the student.

- Consider freezing tuition hikes by buying units of a 529 prepaid tuition plan.

- Give appreciated property to the student; let the student pay the tax, and let the student pay the college expenses.

CASE STUDIES

The Madsen Case

To help you apply this material, we'd like to introduce you to Mary Anne Madsen, who is a widow (age 66). She has three children and five grandchildren. Until recently, she felt barely comfortable financially and not in a position to help with her grandchildren's college needs. However, this changed when she received an unexpected inheritance from a distant relative. She now feels that she can give $30,000 to each of her grandchildren and she would like to ensure that the funds are used for college. The following chart shows her family situation.

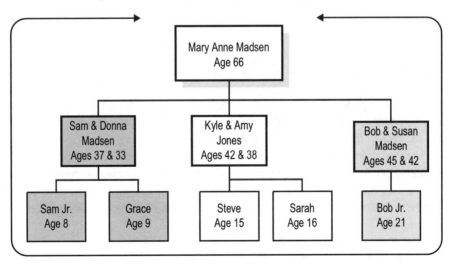

The Madsen Clan

Normally, we would start the planning process with the **College Planning Conversation**. This would give Mary Anne an idea of how large the actual college problem was going to be for her grandchildren and help her decide how much to contribute. In this case, however, Mary Anne has a defined amount to give already in mind. And she doesn't have the luxury of giving more. So we skipped that step and went on to a discussion of the **Family Scholarship Plan**.

Although Mary Anne is not in a very high tax bracket, she still doesn't like to pay taxes. She also wants help managing her investments, but also wants to be kept informed. Mary Anne's desires are simple and are summarized Figure 5.4, **Benefit Evaluation Form**.

Figure 5.4

Benefits Evaluation Form™	**Ranking** 10 = Most Important 1 = Least Important
1 Tax-free growth	7
2 Tax-free distributions	7
3 Investment control	4
4 Distribution control	10
5 Estate planning	4
6 Creditor protection	1
7 Medical planning	1
8 Ability to pay for private elementary and secondary school	1
9 Financial aid availability	1
10 Ability to fund for special needs	1

After completing Mary Anne's Benefit Evaluation Form™, we explained to her that we needed to obtain a similar evaluation from each of her children. We stated that the reason for this was to ensure that Mary Anne's money did the most good, and that we didn't inadvertently create a tax burden for her children or cause her grandchildren to lose any financial aid. She called each of her children, informed them that she was establishing a **Family Scholarship Plan**, and asked them to meet and cooperate with us so that she could maximize the benefits to her grandchildren.

We first met with Bob and Susan Madsen. Bob is Mary Anne's oldest son. Their son, Bob, Jr., was about to enter his senior year at a small, very prestigious, and very expensive liberal arts college. His tuition alone exceeded $30,000. Room, board, and other expenses added more to the total bill. Bob and Susan make good money, but their income had increased substantially only in the last five years. Prior to that, they were still paying off some back debts and were struggling financially. Bob Jr. had not received any financial aid during his previous three years of college and Bob and Susan did not expect any help financial aid-wise during his senior year.

Next we met with Kyle and Amy Jones. Amy is Mary Anne's only daughter. She married Kyle, a teacher. Amy is a stay at home mom. The Jones' current annual family income is under $60,000. Their children, Sarah (age 16) and Steve (age 15) are both excellent students and hope to go to Ivy League schools. The Jones family is hoping for financial aid in order to make their college dreams come true.

Finally, we met with Sam and Donna Madsen. Sam, Mary Anne's youngest son, is a doctor. He and his wife live in Beverly Hills, California. Sam specializes in plastic surgery. He has several up and coming movie stars as clients and is doing very well financially. Sam and Donna met at a small, private, liberal arts college. Both went on to graduate school and they want the same for their children, Grace, age 9, and Sam Jr., age 8. Dr. Sam has almost finished paying off his substantial student loan debt. Sam and Donna have not yet begun a college savings plan for their children.

We completed all of the appropriate diagnostic tests for each of the children and summarized them for Mary Anne in Figure 5.5, the **Family Benefit Consolidation Summary**. Since Mary Anne would not be funding all of the college costs for her grandchildren, the most important of the diagnostic tests involved financial aid eligibility. (We didn't reproduce the **Financial Aid Test** results here to save space.)

As you can see in Figure 5.5, Mary Anne's grandchildren each have substantially different needs. Mary Anne needs three separate and different plans:

For her oldest grandson, Bob Jr., Mary Anne elected a **Direct Pay Plan** by writing a check directly to the college. By doing this, she can give the entire $30,000 without any gift tax complications. Because this is a **Crisis Planning** situation, there is no time to save and, consequently, no reason to set up a savings plan. Since financial aid is not a factor, Mary Anne can pay the college directly and won't impact financial aid negatively. Her contribution will reduce Bob and Susan's financial obligation substantially.

Figure 5.5

	Mary Anne Madsen	Bob & Susan Madsen	Kyle & Amy Jones	Sam & Donna Madsen
Family Benefit Consolidation Summary™ **The Family Scholarship Plan™**				
Students		Bob Jr. (21)	Steve (15) Sarah (16)	Sam (8) Grace (9)
Planning Status		Crisis	Crisis	Long-Term Savings
Tax-free growth	7	1	5	10
Tax-free distributions	7	10	5	10
Investment control	4	1	1	1
Distribution control	10	1	1	1
Estate planning	4	1	1	1
Creditor protection	1	1	1	1
Medical planning	1	1	1	1
Ability to pay for private elementary and secondary school	1	1	1	5
Financial aid availability	1	1	10	1
Ability to fund for special needs	1	1	4	4

College for the Jones' children is not far away and they are also in a **Crisis Planning** situation. For her middle grandchildren, Steve and Sarah, Mary Anne elected to save the money in her own name. Since there is not a lot of time until school starts, the money will be invested conservatively and earnings won't substantially impact Mary Anne's tax situation. The plan is to have the Jones family apply for financial aid. After the aid award is made, Mary Anne will give Kyle and Amy the difference between the college bill and the financial aid award. She will do this each year until the $30,000 plus any earnings she receives is depleted. At that point, the Jones family will have to go it alone. The money will be a gift, not income, and will immediately be paid to the college so it will not show as an asset on the Jones' financial aid applications. Mary Anne hopes this strategy will not hurt Steve's and Sarah's future financial aid possibilities.

Mary Anne's youngest grandchildren, Sam, Jr., age 8, and Grace, age 9, have several years before starting college. So Mary Anne decided to set up a **Long-Term College Savings Plan** using 529 savings plans. She deposited $30,000 into each of the children's accounts, but wondered if her contribution would be meaningful given the high cost schools that Sam and Donna are planning for (Bowdoin College). We ran the "Real" Grandparent Contribution™ so that she could see the impact. In both cases, as indicated below and in Figures 5.6 and 5.7, she will be contributing about 14% of the college bill.

Grandma Madsen's "Real" Grandparent Contribution to Grace and Sam Jr.					
	Projected Total College Costs	Mary Anne's Initial Deposit	Projected Investment Growth @7.5%	The "Real" Grandparent Contribution (dollars)	The "Real" Grandparent Contribution (percentage)
Grace	$398,253	$30,000	$27,517	$57,517	14.44%
Sam Jr.	$429,755	$30,000	$31,831	$61,831	14.39%

As a strategic byproduct of helping Mary Anne deal with college, we were also invited to help Mary Anne with her personal finances. Also, Sam and Donna asked us to help design their own college plans for Sam Jr. and Grace.

The Blossom Case

Jon and Jennifer Blossom live and work in suburban Philadelphia. They have one child, Amy, and two grandchildren, Tom and Sarah (see top of next page). Jim, Amy's husband, is an up-and-coming executive for a small telecommunications company. Grandson Tom is finishing his sophomore year of college and granddaughter Sarah is finishing her senior year of high school. Both grandchildren will be attending the same private college. Tom's first two years of college were paid for by his parents. He was only able to qualify for student loans totaling about $6,000; there was no other financial aid available for him. Jim and Amy drained their cash reserves to pay for Tom's first two years and were somewhat relieved to learn that because there will be two children in college at the same time, Tom and Sarah will each receive substantial financial aid. They have calculated, however, that Sarah will probably not receive much financial aid for her junior and senior years. Jon and Jennifer are ready to help out and feel that they can contribute $100,000 to Tom and Sarah's education.

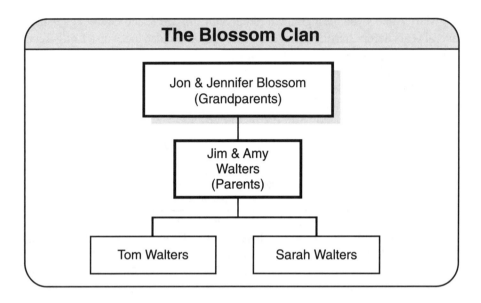

Our diagnostics for the Blossom clan included conducting the **Family Scholarship Plan** and interviews with both Jon and Jennifer and Jim and Amy. As a result we prepared Figure 5.8, the **Family Benefit Consolidation Summary**. In addition, we completed a **Financial Aid Appraisal** (see Figure 5.9).

Although the Blossoms certainly want to generate any tax benefits they can, they are most concerned with relieving some of the financial stress that college was putting on their daughter and son-in-law. **The Financial Aid Test** (not shown) and the **Financial Aid Appraisal** (not shown) demonstrated how significant financial aid might be— more than $38,000 over the next four years. The Blossoms didn't want their planning to jeopardize this much in potential college cash flow. The table below shows total projected college costs and the projected Parent Expected Contribution.

Year	Projected Total College Costs	# Students in College	Projected Parent Expected Contribution
2007	$53,794	2	$36,000
2008	$58,038	2	$37,296
2009	$31,309	1	$38,639*
2010	$33,779	1	$40,040*

*Actual PEC would not exceed actual college costs for year.

Figure 5.6

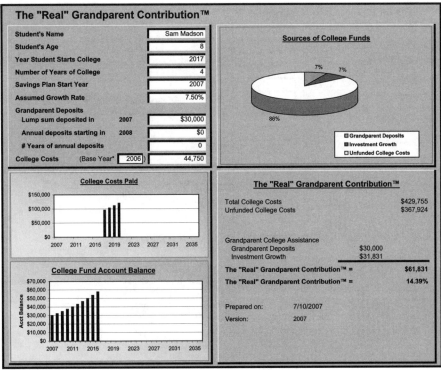

The "Real" Grandparent Contribution™

Student's Name		Sam Madson
Student's Age		8
Year Student Starts College		2017
Number of Years of College		4
Savings Plan Start Year		2007
Assumed Growth Rate		7.50%
Grandparent Deposits		
Lump sum deposited in	2007	$30,000
Annual deposits starting in	2008	$0
# Years of annual deposits		0
College Costs (Base Year* 2006)		44,750

Sources of College Funds

7%   7%

86%

☑ Grandparent Deposits
■ Investment Growth
☐ Unfunded College Costs

College Costs Paid

$150,000
$100,000
$50,000
$0
2007 2011 2015 2019 2023 2027 2031 2035

College Fund Account Balance

$70,000
$60,000
$50,000
$40,000
$30,000
$20,000
$10,000
$0
Acct Balance
2007 2011 2015 2019 2023 2027 2031 2035

The "Real" Grandparent Contribution™

Total College Costs	$429,755
Unfunded College Costs	$367,924

Grandparent College Assistance		
Grandparent Deposits	$30,000	
Investment Growth	$31,831	
The "Real" Grandparent Contribution™ =		$61,831
The "Real" Grandparent Contribution™ =		14.39%

Prepared on:	7/10/2007
Version:	2007

*2006 – 2007

Figure 5.7

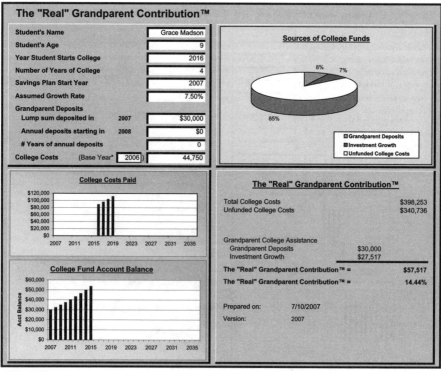

The "Real" Grandparent Contribution™

Student's Name	Grace Madson
Student's Age	9
Year Student Starts College	2016
Number of Years of College	4
Savings Plan Start Year	2007
Assumed Growth Rate	7.50%

Grandparent Deposits

Lump sum deposited in	2007	$30,000
Annual deposits starting in	2008	$0
# Years of annual deposits		0
College Costs (Base Year* 2006)		44,750

Sources of College Funds

8% 7% 85%

☐ Grandparent Deposits
■ Investment Growth
☐ Unfunded College Costs

College Costs Paid

$120,000
$100,000
$80,000
$60,000
$40,000
$20,000
$0

2007 2011 2015 2019 2023 2027 2031 2035

The "Real" Grandparent Contribution™

Total College Costs	$398,253
Unfunded College Costs	$340,736

Grandparent College Assistance
Grandparent Deposits	$30,000
Investment Growth	$27,517

The "Real" Grandparent Contribution™ =	$57,517
The "Real" Grandparent Contribution™ =	14.44%

Prepared on:	7/10/2007
Version:	2007

College Fund Account Balance

$60,000
$50,000
$40,000
$30,000
$20,000
$10,000
$0

Acct Balance

2007 2011 2015 2019 2023 2027 2031 2035

*2006 – 2007

Figure 5.8

Family Benefit Consolidation Summary™			
	Grandparent Data	**Student Data**	**Student Data**
Names/age	Jon & Jennifer	Tom	Sarah
Planning Status		Crisis	Crisis
Tax-free growth	8	10	10
Tax-free distributions	8	10	10
Investment control	2	0	0
Distribution control	8	0	0
Estate planning	2	0	0
Creditor protection	2	0	0
Medical planning	2	0	0
Ability to pay for private elementary and secondary school	0	0	0
Financial aid availability	8	8	8 - yrs 1, 2 0 - yrs 3, 4
Ability to fund for special needs	0	0	0

The following outline is the solution the Blossoms implemented:

• **Part 1: Sarah's freshman and sophomore years and Tom's junior and senior years (2008 and 2009)**

The Blossoms plan to give $24,000 per year to Tom and Sarah's parents after the financial aid award has been made in 2008 and 2009. The Blossoms will instruct the parents to use the money to immediately pay college bills.

  • This strategy should not adversely impact Tom or Sarah's financial aid eligibility:

    • The funds are a gift and are not taxable income to either the parents or the students.

    • The funds will not be considered an "asset" when the next years' financial aid forms are completed because they will already have been spent.

Figure 5.9

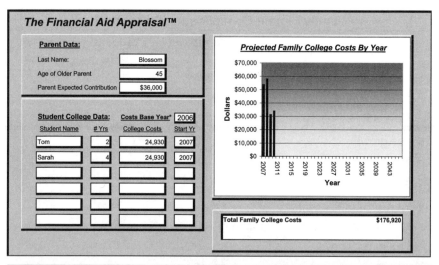

The Financial Aid Appraisal™

Parent Data:

Last Name:	Blossom
Age of Older Parent	45
Parent Expected Contribution	$36,000

Student College Data:		Costs Base Year*	2006
Student Name	# Yrs	College Costs	Start Yr
Tom	2	24,930	2007
Sarah	4	24,930	2007

Projected Family College Costs By Year

Total Family College Costs	$176,920

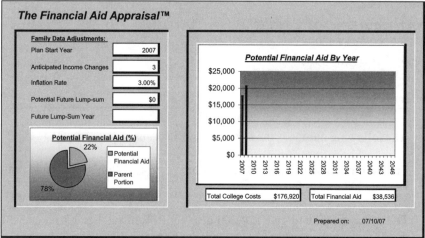

The Financial Aid Appraisal™

Family Data Adjustments:

Plan Start Year	2007
Anticipated Income Changes	3
Inflation Rate	3.00%
Potential Future Lump-sum	$0
Future Lump-Sum Year	

Potential Financial Aid (%)

22% Potential Financial Aid
78% Parent Portion

Potential Financial Aid By Year

Total College Costs	$176,920	Total Financial Aid	$38,536

Prepared on: 07/10/07

This program is designed to help families plan for future college expenditures. It projects future college costs and future financial aid eligibility based on current and past college cost data and current financial aid formulas which can change substantially over time. **This program is intended for planning purposes only and implies no guarantees.**

Projecting college costs and financial aid can be useful in the planning process to help decide on savings commitments and college funding vehicles. But for best results, projections should be recalculated annually using the most current version of this spreadsheet.

Version: 2007

*2006 – 2007

- This strategy should not impact Tom and Sarah's parents' income tax situation. The funds represent a gift to the parents, not taxable income.

- This strategy has no significant tax effect on the grandparents:

  - There are no gift taxes. The gift is under the $12,000 gift tax annual exclusion and qualifies as a gift of a present interest.

  - There will be minimum interest income and, therefore, minimum taxes due on the $24,000 gift that is deferred to 2009.

- **Part 2: Sarah's Junior and Senior Years (2010 and 2011):**

Immediately open a 529 prepaid tuition plan for Sarah's last two years of college. The purpose is to effectively lock-in today's tuition rates. The Blossoms chose The Independent 529 Plan, a non state-specific plan since Tom and Sarah's private college is a participating member school. The Blossoms contributed $48,000 to the plan accounts. They will need to wait three years (Sarah's senior year of high school, and her freshman and sophomore years of college) before they can make a withdrawal for Sarah. The plan owners are the grandparents; the plan beneficiary is Sarah. Eligible expenses for payment from this plan are tuition and fees only.

- This plan effectively freezes any tuition and fee increases for Sarah's junior and senior years. It also provides the funds to pay these expenses so that Sarah's parents don't need to worry about them. However, Sarah's parents will still need to cover other expenses, including room and board.

- This plan should not affect either Sarah's or Tom's financial aid. The plan values are not an asset of either student or their parents. There will be no distributions from the plan during Sarah's first two years of college, when the Blossoms want to guard against financial aid loss.

- The plan will have no effect on Sarah's parents' tax situation. They have no ownership and no control over the plan. They simply are not involved with the plan.

- The plan has a positive tax impact:

  - There are no gift taxes because of the gift tax annual exclusion allowed for 529 plan contributions.

- When a distribution is made to Sarah, there will be no tax consequences as long as the money is used for qualified education expenses.

Other Grandparent Case Studies

There are several grandparent illustrations examined throughout this text. Each cases study shows different examples of what grandparents have done. But in each case, the *process* was the same:

- Determine the amount that the grandparents will contribute. Often this means taking the grandparents through the **College Planning Conversation** to show them the magnitude of the college problem and to get them to realize just how important their contribution is going to be.

- Discuss the **Family Scholarship Plan** with the grandparents, focusing on benefits not tools.

- Obtain an introduction to the children to ensure that college funds are set up appropriately.

- Discuss the **Family Scholarship Plan** with the children. Pay particular attention to the planning time horizon (long-term plan or crisis plan). Although all the benefits on the list are important, pay particular attention to financial aid eligibility. It will have a major impact on tool choice and account titling.

- Show the grandparent the **"Real" Grandparent Contribution** to reinforce the degree of value they are providing to their grandchildren.

- If appropriate, and if you have permission of the grandparent to divulge the grandparent contribution, have the **College Planning Conversation** with the children. This can generate appreciation for the grandparent contribution and get the parents motivated to add to the plan.

For other grandparent ideas, you may wish to refer to the following cases:

- The case of Chuck and Ann (Chapter 2) demonstrates that different approaches were necessary for different grandchildren, because parents' financial circumstances were different.

- The case of Mort and Sylvia (Chapter 2) demonstrates a grandparent plan using only interest from an investment to help with student spending money.

- Grandpa Bill's case (Chapter 2) shows how to execute a "match" plan.

Chapter 6

TOOLS & RULES FOR LONG-TERM COLLEGE SAVINGS

The purpose of Chapters 6, 7, and 8 is to give you the tools and rules you need to create successful college plans for your clients, whether they have time to save or whether they're in crisis mode. In keeping with the format of processes as outlined in these chapters, the balance of this chapter will start with long-term savings plan tools followed by crisis planning tools. Note that several of our College Money diagnostic tools have applications in long-term savings plan design as well as in crisis planning. To avoid confusion, we will discuss those tools at the end of this chapter.

When it comes to saving for college, there are numerous choices of appropriate savings vehicles. The purpose of this chapter is to give a general overview of the most popular choices along with sources for more specific information.

No single college savings tool is always right for every client. Selection of a tool should be made after a discussion with the client to determine the benefit(s) that he or she would like to build-in to the plan.

529 PLANS

Perhaps one of the most recognized savings tools is the 529 plan (qualified tuition program), which encompasses two categories: prepaid plans and savings plans. Both types of plans were instituted by the federal government to be administered by individual states. The federal rules are general; states will superimpose their own rules on their own plans. For that reason, it is important to read the plan document of the particular state's plan being considered.

The rules for 529 plans include:

- 529 plans can only accept cash contributions.

- Coverdell Education Savings Accounts, Series EE and Series I savings bonds, and the cash proceeds of UGMA/UTMA accounts are all considered acceptable rollover contributions to a 529 plan.

- Investors cannot make day-to-day investment decisions on the plans, but can reallocate once in a 12-month period.

- The custodian of the account can change the beneficiary to certain other family members; however, there may be generation-skipping tax implications.

- Anyone can own a 529 plan for himself or herself.

- There is no federal tax deduction for contributions to a 529 plan.

- Withdrawals are federal income-tax free if used for qualified education expenses.

- Donors can prepay up to five years of contributions under the annual gift tax exclusion. In 2007, that amount is $60,000, or $12,000 per year, per beneficiary. The contribution is considered a completed gift; however as custodian of the 529 account, the contributor can take the money back at any time (subject to taxes and a 10% penalty on the growth). Furthermore, if the contributor dies during the 5-year period, the equivalent of the remaining years' contribution is added back to his or her estate.

- There are also accommodations for students with 529 plans who receive a scholarship, become disabled, or die. If there is no other beneficiary to roll the benefits over to, the custodian can withdraw the funds with taxes due, but no penalty.

- Federal financial aid treatment of 529 plans has become much more favorable in recent years. The financial aid system will consider the balance of the account to be a parental asset when calculating need-based financial aid eligibility. When the custodian or student requests a withdrawal to pay for qualified education expenses, the gain is not deemed income to the student or to the custodian.

529 Prepaid Tuition Plans

A prepaid tuition plan is a type of 529 college savings plan designed to allow families to pay the equivalent of tomorrow's state college tuition at today's rates. However it is not quite as simple as that. There are two types of pre-paid tuition plans: unit plans and contract plans. The unit plans sell a fixed percentage of tuition. Once a unit is purchased, the percentage value remains the same as it was when it was originally purchased, regardless how the price of a unit may have changed from year to year.

Contract plans, on the other hand, require participants to agree to purchase a specified number of years' worth of tuition and mandatory fees. Some state plans may also include the cost of room and board, but most do not. The cost will depend on (1) the number of years until the student begins college, (2) whether the payment will be lump sum or installment, and (3) the number of years purchased.

It is important to recognize that each prepaid tuition plan will vary from state to state. Some plans offer guarantees backed by the full faith and credit of the state, while others offer a statutory guarantee. Investors should be sure of the nature of the guarantee because a market downturn could affect their plan. In recent years, some states felt compelled to close their prepaid plans to new investors because they were concerned that they might not be able to meet their obligation based on market conditions.

Maximum contribution limits vary by state. Generally plans will allow up to five years' tuition and fees. There are no income limits for contributors.

Most states do not restrict students to attending an in-state college in order to use that state's benefits. If a student chooses to attend a private college or an out-of-state college, they will receive the equivalent of the state college tuition and fees of their state.

For more detailed information about 529 prepaid tuition plans, consult the plan document of the individual state being considered. Additional information sources can be found at the end of this section.

Independent 529 Plan

Several years ago, a consortium of colleges instituted a prepaid plan not specifically affiliated with a state called The Independent 529 Plan. Under this plan (administered by TIAA-CREF), member colleges guarantee the tuition benefit at a discounted rate (.5% minimum); some colleges offer a higher discount. Investors do not have to "choose" a specific college. Rather they are locking in the tuition costs at all the participating colleges. The percentage of costs locked in will depend on the costs and discount offered at a specific college. When a student receives acceptance at a member college, their parents can redeem their certificate for that college.

There are, however, issues that make this plan complicated and perhaps less desirable to investors. First, investors in the Independent 529 Plan will have a difficult time knowing how their plan is performing. Although the plan will track five colleges of the investor's choice annually to give them an idea of the percentage of costs their investment would cover, it really is irrelevant because if the student is only two years old, the parents have no idea where the child will ultimately go to college. The child might not end up at one of the five colleges at all.

A second issue is that the pool of participating colleges is very limited. This factor has a major impact on the investment returns. As mentioned earlier, if the beneficiary is two years old, what are the odds that he or she will go to one of the 250 schools on the list? If the child does attend one of the participating schools, the return on investment will be a combination of college inflation plus the discount the school offers (at least .5%). For example, if college inflation averaged 5% and the college offered a .5% discount on tuition and fees, then the family's return would be 5.5%. But what if the child chooses a nonparticipating school, or doesn't go to college at all? The return is the principal plus or minus 2%.

Assuming there is a pool of 2,500 possible colleges in the country, and that 250 of these colleges are participating in the Independent 529 Plan, there is a 10% chance the student will attend one of the 250 schools, and a 90% chance that he or she won't. In other words, there is a 10% chance of a return of college inflation plus the discount and a 90% chance of a return of plus or minus 2%. Not very attractive numbers!

Waiting until the student is in high school to invest in the plan does improve the odds. The parents know the student better and can review the list with the student to evaluate potential schools. Using a strategy of investing in a 529 savings plan's age-based portfolio, and then transferring the account to the Independent 529 Plan when the child is in high school (and the age-based portfolio is about to switch to bonds and cash) might make more sense. However, there is a 3-year waiting period on accepting distributions from the Independent 529 Plan, so the matter becomes complicated once again. Should the parents liquidate all at once and dump the proceeds into the Independent 529 Plan? Or should they liquidate one year at a time and be sure to start early enough to avoid getting caught in the waiting period? The answer will depend on individual circumstances.

For more specific information, visit The Independent 529 Plan website at: www.independent529plan.org.

529 Savings Plans

The second type of 529 plan is a savings plan. Under this plan, a contributor is not limited to saving for tuition and mandatory fees only because "qualified education expenses" are defined more loosely to include books, room and board, and special equipment required by the school. For example, if a course of study requires uniforms or a computer, these items can fall under the definition of "qualified education expense."

A second difference between 529 savings plans and prepaid tuition plans is that the savings plans participate in market returns. Where prepaid plans are pegged to the college tuition and fees for a particular state, a savings plan will generate returns based on market performance. Investors should understand that this means if the market goes up, their account values will go up. Conversely, if the market goes down, their account value could go down as well.

529 savings plans can also be used for graduate school, whereas prepaid plans tend to be designed for undergraduate school. Anyone can have a 529 savings plan for himself, which can be a boon for adults who opt for a second career later in life.

As with prepaid plans, there is no federal tax deduction for contributions to savings plans, but if the funds are used for qualified education expenses, the growth portion of the distribution is federal income-tax free. Most states follow suit with respect to the latter. Some states offer state income tax deductions on all or part of the contribution amount. More recently, Pennsylvania passed legislation that allows residents to take a state income tax deduction for contributions made to *any* state's 529 plan, not just the Pennsylvania TAP plan. More states will probably follow suit.

Maximum contribution limits vary from state to state, but are usually very generous. Some state limits are as high as $300,000 per student for all accounts in that state. The rule is that once the account value reaches the specified limit, no additional contributions are permitted. The intention is that account values should not exceed the highest cost of college in that state.

Investment options in 529 savings plans usually include age-based portfolios, static portfolios, and/or individual portfolios. The age-based portfolios are designed to adjust the mix of stocks, bonds, and cash as the student's age increases. These plans are designed to be more aggressive in the child's younger years and more conservative as the child gets closer to college age. Static portfolios have a fixed percentage of stocks to bonds, and the individual portfolios allow the investor to delineate their own investment strategy. However, it is important to remember that the federal rules generally allow an investor to reallocate their portfolios only once in a 12-month period.

Again, it is imperative that advisors review the plan document for specific state features and rules when recommending these tools to their clients. Some states offer tax incentives, and others may have restrictions on who can participate.

COVERDELL EDUCATION SAVINGS ACCOUNTS

Coverdell Education Savings Accounts (ESAs) were created by EGTRRA 2001 to replace the Education IRA. The changes enacted by this law made a heretofore so-so savings vehicle much more attractive, and included:

- an increase of the maximum contribution amount from $500 annually to $2,000;

- the addition of elementary and secondary education expenses to the definition of qualified education expenses;

- increases in the income phase-out limits for those married, joint filers; and

- improvements in the coordination with 529 plans and the education tax credits.

(Please note that although the Pension Protection Act of 2006 removed the sunset provisions on 529 plans, it did not do so for Coverdell Education Savings Accounts. Therefore the changes listed above are scheduled to expire on December 31, 2010.)

The current rules for Coverdell ESAs include the following:

- The beneficiary must be under age 18 when the account is opened.

- Contributions must be cash, are not tax deductible, and must be made by the due date of the contributor's tax return (not including extensions, usually April 15).

- Contributions to a Coverdell ESA are limited by the income of the contributor. For single filers, the ability to contribute begins to phase-out at $95,000 per year and is completely eliminated at $110,000. Joint filers begin to phase-out at $190,000 and can no longer contribute when their income reaches $220,000.

- Corporations can contribute to an individual's Coverdell ESA regardless of income level. The contribution will be reported as income.

- Contributions cannot exceed a total of $2,000 in any year for *all* accounts of a single beneficiary.

- No contributions can be made once the beneficiary reaches age 18 (unless the beneficiary is a special needs beneficiary).

- The account must be used before the beneficiary reaches age 30 (unless the beneficiary is a special needs beneficiary). If the account is not used, a distribution must be taken (subject to taxes and penalties) unless the account is rolled over to a younger beneficiary.

- "Qualified education expenses" for elementary and secondary schools include tuition and fees, books, supplies, and equipment, academic tutoring, and special needs services for a special needs beneficiary.

  - In order to constitute a "qualified" expense, certain expenses must be required or provided by an eligible elementary or secondary school in connection with attendance or enrollment at the school. Those expenses include room and board, uniforms, transportation, and supplementary items and services (including extended day programs). Computer technology, equipment, or Internet access and related services are deemed qualified elementary and secondary education expenses if they are to be used by the beneficiary and the beneficiary's family during any of the years the beneficiary is in elementary or secondary school. *Caution*: Expenses for computer software designed for sports, games, or hobbies are *not* allowed unless the software is predominantly educational in nature.

- "Qualified education expenses" for post-secondary schools must be required for enrollment or attendance of a designated beneficiary at an eligible postsecondary school. They include tuition and fees, books, supplies, and equipment.

  - Expenses for special needs services needed by a special needs beneficiary must be incurred in connection with enrollment or attendance at an eligible postsecondary school.

  - Expenses for room and board must be incurred by students who are enrolled at least half-time. The expense for room and board qualifies only to the extent that it is not more than the greater of the following two amounts: (1) the allowance for room and board, as determined by the school, that was included in the cost of attendance (for federal financial aid purposes) for a particular academic period and living arrangement of the student; *or* (2) the actual amount charged if the student is residing in housing owned or operated by the school.

- Any contribution from a Coverdell ESA to a 529 plan must be on behalf of the designated beneficiary of the Coverdell ESA *or*, in the case of a change in beneficiary, a family member of the designated beneficiary.

- Contributions can be made without penalty to a Coverdell ESA and a 529 plan in the same year for the same beneficiary.

- The Hope Scholarship Credit or Lifetime Learning Credit can be claimed in the same year the beneficiary takes a tax-free distribution from a Coverdell ESA as long as the same expenses are not used for both benefits. This means the beneficiary must reduce qualified higher education expenses by tax-free educational assistance, and then further reduce those expenses by any expenses taken into account in determining a Hope Scholarship Credit or Lifetime Learning Credit.

- If a designated beneficiary receives distributions from a Coverdell ESA and a 529 plan in the same year, and the total distribution total more than the beneficiary's adjusted qualified higher education expenses, those expenses must be allocated between the distribution from the Coverdell ESA and the distribution from the 529 plan before figuring how much of each distribution is taxable.

- As of the writing of this book, a specific definition for "special needs" has not been published. However, when drafting the legislation for Coverdell ESA, the committee recommended that the term "special needs" should include "an individual who because of a physical, mental, or emotional condition (including learning disability) requires additional time to complete his or her education."

UGMA/UTMA ACCOUNTS

Uniform Gifts to Minors Accounts (UGMA) and Uniform Transfers to Minors Accounts (UTMA) were once the primary tax-favored savings vehicles for children's education. Over time, and due to changes in the law concerning the taxation of children's unearned income, however they have become less attractive. Here are the basic rules. A custodian opens an account for a child using the child's Social Security number. Deposits to the account are considered completed gifts to the child and cannot be taken back. During the child's minor years, the custodian controls the account and makes investment decisions. The custodian may make withdrawals from the account, but the withdrawals must be used for the benefit of the child. Parents may not use the funds for any expenses that can be deemed parental responsibility (e.g., food, shelter, and clothing). However the funds can be used for nonessential items such as private school tuition, computers, cars and car insurance, class trips, etc.

The attraction of these accounts was twofold. First, for parents who were concerned about their child's college savings being exposed to lawsuits and creditors because of their profession, the UGMA/UTMA was a safe place because it was the property of the child and, as such, was not available. Secondly, the accounts were tax-favored, giving parents a tax break. Originally, earnings were taxed at the child's usually lower rate. Later, the tax rules were changed to protect earnings up to a specific amount and then an equal amount was taxed at the child's lower rate, with anything above that being taxed to the parents. Once the child reached age 14 under prior law, all earnings were taxed at the child's rate, which is usually lower than the parents' tax rate. In 2006, however, the age limit was raised to 18; in 2007, the limit was raised again to age 19. These changes effectively eliminated the tax benefit for these accounts as college savings accounts.

Another disadvantage to using UGMA/UTMA accounts had to do with the ownership of the accounts. As stated earlier, contributions to the accounts are completed gifts and become the property of the child. Once the child reaches the age of majority (18 in many states), he or she can take custody of the account. While in most cases found the funds were used for college as the parents had intended, there were instances however where the child took control of the funds, never used the money for college, and the parents had no legal recourse.

Finally, UGMA/UTMA accounts are treated unfavorably by the financial aid system. These accounts are owned by the student; therefore, the asset is assessed at a higher rate under the formulas than the parental assets. In addition, when distributions are taken, if there is a taxable gain it will also increase the student's income, further reducing available financial aid.

Strategies for families that already have UGMA/UTMA accounts but want to make the best of the situation include:

- Cash in the account, pay the taxes, and open a UGMA/UTMA - 529 Plan. The funds retain the UGMA/UTMA characteristics so the account still belongs to the child. The account will enjoy tax-free growth and there will be spending disincentives (in the form of the 10% penalty, if the student uses the funds for a sports car instead of college). Moreover, the United States Department of Education has further stipulated that a UGMA/UTMA - 529 Plan will not be considered a student asset, making it additionally attractive.

- During the pre-college years, spend down the account on items that are for the benefit of the student (e.g., a computer, senior trip, prom, private school tuition, a car, and automobile insurance, etc.). However don't just make that money disappear without replacing it. If the items were things the parent would have ordinarily paid for, then the parent can use the student's money and put an equivalent amount into a 529 account.

UNITED STATES SERIES EE OR SERIES I SAVINGS BONDS

United States savings bonds interest can be tax-free if used to pay educational expenses, but only under specific limitations:

- The bond owner must be age 24 or older when the bond is purchased.

- The bond must be registered in the bond owner's name (or the bond owner's and spouse's names).

- "Qualified education expenses" include tuition and mandatory fees, or a contribution to a 529 plan or a Coverdell ESA. Room and board is *not* considered to be a qualified education expense.

- The income phase-out limitations surrounding the use of Series EE or Series I bonds for college in 2007 are:

  - Married, filing jointly - $98,400 - $128,400

  - Single or Head of Household - $65,600 - $80,600

  - Married, filing separately – not eligible

- *Strategy*: If your client is approaching the income phase-out, consider cashing in the bonds and moving them to a 529 Plan. A contribution to a 529 plan is considered a qualified education expense and would, therefore, render the bond interest tax-free.

LIFE INSURANCE

As a savings tool for college, life insurance is a valid option. A parent can overload the cash value of the policy and, with careful planning, when the time for college comes take the money out of the policy on a tax-free basis. The initial policy withdrawals can be return of premiums. Subsequent to that, policy loans can be used. However, there are several caveats:

- Although life insurance cash values are not considered in the federal financial aid calculations, colleges are not required to use the federal formula when awarding their own college funds for financial aid. Colleges can ask any questions they want, and often do ask about life insurance products. Using insurance purely for the purpose of "beating" the financial aid system is not recommended.

- When using policy loans, the policy owner must be careful to leave enough cash in the policy to keep it in force. The policy must mature and result in a death claim in order for the withdrawals to remain tax-free.

- Unless there is a need for insurance, it may not be the optimal choice for maximum savings. Because the cost of insurance must be factored into the return on investment, a 529 plan might be a better alternative.

- Using life insurance as a tool to hide assets from the financial aid system can backfire. Please see the sidebar in Chapter 7 about asset-repositioning.

A final comment on using life insurance as a college savings vehicle pertains to the creation of a grandparent college savings plan. When working with grandparents, there may be a reason to use life insurance. Remember the story of Chuck and Ann Sample (Chapter 2)? They were delighted to be able to insure their son-in-law's life while saving for their grandchildren's college years. Life insurance solved two issues for the Samples: (1) they could save for college on a tax-free basis; and (2) they were protecting their daughter and her children in the event of the early demise of their son-in-law.

OTHER INVESTMENTS

Some parents don't want to be restricted in their savings. While it might be appealing to take advantage of the tax-free nature of the federal college savings plans, if the money is not used for college the parents may not want to pay a penalty. Therefore, a portfolio of mutual funds may be the appropriate choice in these situations.

As an advisor, it is your responsibility to allocate the mutual funds to maximize the returns in the early years and gradually shift the allocation to a more conservative stance as college approaches. To minimize taxes, the advisor should consider tax-free municipal bonds as a segment of the portfolio.

When constructing any portfolio, it is important to factor in college inflation. A portfolio that is very conservative might not grow enough to meet the college needs of the family. This puts added pressure on them to save larger amounts early in the game at a time when they might not have the disposable cash to do so.

IRAs and College Savings

Individual retirement accounts (IRAs) can also be used as a college savings tool. Basically, withdrawals used for qualified higher education expenses are penalty-free, but taxes are payable on the growth component. Because contributions to Roth IRAs are made with after-tax dollars, Roth IRAs provide the additional benefit that withdrawals up to the amount of the contributions can be taken out first, tax-free. As with traditional IRAs, withdrawals of the growth portion from a Roth IRA will be taxable, but penalty-free.

Because college financing can quickly become a retirement problem if parents are not careful, advisors should exercise caution when recommending that parents use their retirement funds to pay for college. If IRAs make up a significant share of their retirement nest egg, they need to be very careful about jeopardizing their retirement by using those funds to pay for college.

The same caution should also be used when considering a 401(k) plan loan to help pay for college. There are traps to be aware of when dipping in to a 401(k) for college:

- Most 401(k) plans allow up to 50% of the balance of an employee's account to be taken as a "hardship" loan (college qualifies as a "hardship"). However, 401(k) plans usually demand that any loans be paid back within five years. Consequently, if a loan is not paid back on time, the distribution is characterized as a premature withdrawal with taxes and penalties are due.

- Although some persons might argue that by taking a loan from a 401(k), the employee is simply borrowing from himself and paying himself back, what they often don't realize is that they've lost the benefit of tax-free growth on those funds. They can't just "put that back."

The same comments would also apply with respect to using retirement money, generally, to pay for college. Typically parents are nearing retirement age at the same time they are struggling with college bills. By using retirement funds to pay for college, they could find themselves with little time to replenish retirement accounts before they need to start drawing income from those same funds.

RESOURCES

www.collegesavings.org

College Savings Plans Network, an affiliate of the National Association of State Treasurers. This site offers links to each state's 529 plans.

http://www.irs.gov/pub/irs-pdf/p970.pdf

Internal Revenue Service Publication 970 (Tax Benefits for Education)

www.msrb.org

Municipal Securities Rulemaking Board (which regulates the sale of 529 plans).

www.nasdr.org

National Association of Securities Dealers (which regulates broker-dealers).

www.ed.gov

United States Department of Education

Chapter 7

TOOLS & RULES FOR CRISIS COLLEGE PLANS

NEED-BASED FINANCIAL AID RULES

Congress has devised a federal financial aid system that includes a complex calculation designed to determine an amount that a family can afford to pay in a given year toward the cost of college. This amount, called the Expected Family Contribution (EFC), is then compared to the cost of the college the student has applied to. If the cost of the college is higher than the EFC, the student has demonstrated that he or she "needs" financial assistance. On the other hand, if the cost of college is less than the EFC, then under the system the family has not demonstrated that the student needs financial assistance in order to attend that college. The Federal Methodology, as it is called, is used for determining eligibility for financial aid from federal sources (and often for state financial aid as well).

A Word about Asset Repositioning to Wrangle More Financial Aid

Because the Federal Methodology does not include retirement assets, life insurance cash values, or annuities in the asset calculation, some advisors recommend that parents move some of their assets into one of these types of products in order to lower their assets and qualify for more financial aid.

This can be a dangerous practice and should be considered very carefully before suggesting it. The reason is that although the Institutional Methodology does not include these products in the basic calculation, there is still "Section Q" to deal with. Section Q is a part of the Institutional Methodology where individual colleges can ask additional questions. Some questions we have seen are:

- What is the balance in your parents' 401(k), profit sharing plan, money purchase pension, etc.?

- Do your parents own any annuities? If yes, what is the balance?

- List any cash value life insurance your parents own and the amount of cash value in the policy.

Unless you know in advance exactly what questions will be asked by the colleges your clients' student is applying to, it is risky to put their money into a product that may have a surrender charge or a contingent deferred sales charge. If the question is asked, and the family doesn't receive the financial aid they were counting on, you could lose a client and face suitability questions. And legal action is not outside the realm of possibility either.

Schools have the option of using any method they want when giving out their own funds. Some schools use the Federal Methodology and some employ a second calculation called the Institutional Methodology. And some colleges use a hybrid formula they develop themselves. Advisors and parents need to be aware of the existence of this second formula (i.e., the Institutional Methodology). More importantly, parents need to understand that while some strategies they hear about might garner them more *federal* financial aid, there is no guarantee that the strategy will work when it comes to qualifying for a college's *institutional* financial aid. Since most federal financial aid is in the form of loans, and because most of the "free money" comes through college and university endowment funds, it is important to shop for schools carefully if financial aid is a critical part of the picture.

Sadly, most parents' estimates of what they can afford to pay for college are usually much lower than what the system thinks they can pay. There are several reasons for this.

- The system is slanted to help extremely low income families.

- The system will not give consideration to consumer debt in the form of credit cards or auto loans. Congress believes that the system should not subsidize lifestyle choices.

- The system expects parents to take on debt as part of the educational funding. Therefore the calculations are designed around that expectation.

This book is not intended to be a definitive source on the financial aid system. Therefore, the following overview is a very simplistic explanation for a complicated formula. Basically, the financial aid calculation is comprised of four components:

1. parent income;

2.   parent assets;

3.   student income; and

4.   student assets.

There are various deductions that are applied to these four components. Then a percentage of each is taken and added together to arrive at the EFC. These percentages are:

Federal Methodology	Component	Institutional Methodology
47%	Parent Income	46%
5.6%	Parent Assets	3% - 5%
50%	Student Income	50%
20%	Student Assets	25%

Keep in mind that these percentages are applied *after* deductions and should *not* be applied to gross income and asset figures. In addition, the income component is a graduated table similar to tax tables. Furthermore, the Federal Methodology and the Institutional Methodology differ not only in the structure of the formula, but in some of the allowances as well.

FINANCIAL AID AND DIVORCE

Many people are surprised to learn that a divorced and remarried parent is expected to include the stepparent's financial information on the financial aid forms. The thought process behind this rule is that the custodial parent has additional income coming into the household; therefore, more of his/her income and assets will available for college. For divorced families where both parents have remarried, this philosophy could pull all four parents/stepparents into the mix.

This result may seem unfair because a stepparent does not have a legal responsibility to educate a stepchild. But the financial aid rules are not intended to place legal responsibility; rather, the purpose of the rules is to assess the financial strength of the household. Parents and advisors should be aware that having a noncustodial parent refuse to provide financial information will not necessarily work to the student's advantage. Some colleges might impute income to that parent and then base their decision for college sourced financial aid on those figures.

The financial aid formulas are very complex and go beyond the scope of this book. The Federal financial aid formula and tables are available on the Department of Education website for those advisors who would like to learn more.

SCHOLARSHIP SEARCH

There are stories in the media every year about enterprising students who paid for their entire college career by winning obscure scholarships. While these students are to be congratulated, the reality is that there are very few students who are motivated enough to pursue this option. It is hard work and very time-consuming. The following factors should also be taken into account:

- Many of these scholarships are contests and require an essay, something many students find a torture to write.

- Most of these scholarships are provided for one year only, so the student must apply for them year after year.

- If a student does qualify for need-based financial aid, these scholarships can reduce the amount of financial aid the student would otherwise receive. The financial aid system considers these scholarships as an "outside resource available to pay for college," and also considers these funds an addition to the EFC. Because the system is structured so that the family is supposed to come up with the EFC, the scholarship is added to what the family is contributing to the cost of college, thus reducing the college's financial aid responsibility by an equal amount.

Another favorite of the media is the story about the thousands of dollars of scholarships that go unclaimed every year. While this may in fact be true, there are some other things that parents and students need to understand. These scholarships are often quite restricted. They might be available to students applying only to a specific college. Or they might require that a student be of a specific ethnic origin. They might even go so far as to say the student has to have red hair or be a left-handed tennis player. So, again, it is important to get the whole story before recommending that students get on the scholarship search websites.

Suppose then, that an advisor determines through a financial aid test that a client's student won't qualify for need-based financial aid, isn't a good prospect for merit aid, and is generally an average kid. Should the advisor suggest a scholarship search? If the student is motivated to do the work, a scholarship search can't hurt as long as the parents aren't counting on money that might not materialize. There are websites that will conduct scholarship searches for a student. Here are a couple of caveats concerning these scholarship search services:

1. There is no reason to pay for a scholarship search. There are several reputable sites that do them for free (advertisers subsidize the cost of the website).

2. Often these searches list resources the family already knows about (e.g., Stafford Loans).

Scholarship search engines can be found at:

- Princeton Review: www.princetonreview.com

- FastWeb: www.fastweb.com

- College Board: www.collegeboard.com

CASH FLOW PLANNING

May of a student's senior year of high school is typically the end of the application and acceptance process. The student has received all of the acceptance and rejection letters, and the parents have received the proposed financial aid awards from the accepting colleges. A final decision has been made concerning which school the student will attend, the deposit has been sent in to hold the student's seat in the freshman class, and now it is time for the parents to figure out exactly how they're going to pay the bill that will be arriving sometime in July.

Families that qualify for need-based financial aid must be very careful about liquidating assets in order to pay their part of the bill. If the liquidation generates capital gains, then the gain will have to be shown as income on the next year's financial aid application and could lower the family's financial aid award for that year. However, if parents are taking a distribution from a 529 plan, the distribution should be tax-free and should not affect the Federal Methodology calculation.

Another cash flow strategy is to check to see whether the college offers a monthly payment plan. Most colleges have a plan that allows parents to pay on a monthly basis for 8 - 10 months for a small participation fee. Sometimes being able to break the payments up makes it easier to work the college bill into the parents' monthly cash flow.

LOANS

If savings and regular cash flow aren't sufficient, then most parents will turn to loans. There are *student* loans and *parent* loans to consider. These loans might come from state, federal, or private sources. Many states offer low-interest education loans and grants as an incentive to keep students in-state for college in hopes that the students will settle there after graduation. For purposes of this book, we will discuss only federal loan sources and leave it to the advisor to research state resources appropriate to their clients.

Student Loans

In order of priority, consider subsidized Stafford Loans first. These loans are part of the Federal Title IV loan program and are available for students who have qualified for need-based aid. The federal government will pay the interest on these loans while the student is in college and during a six-month grace period after the student graduates.

However, if a student doesn't qualify for need-based financial aid, they can still get an unsubsidized Stafford Loan. Unsubsidized Stafford Loans are the same as the subsidized loans, except that the interest is not paid by the government; instead, the interest begins to accrue to the loan immediately. Payment on the loan can be deferred until after the student leaves school. All Stafford loans are the sole responsibility of the student; parents do not have to co-sign. The amounts that the student can borrow are modest, but helpful:

- Freshman year: $3,500

- Sophomore year: $4,500

- Junior year: $5,500

- Senior year: $5,500

The interest rates on Subsidized and Unsubsidized Stafford Loans are fixed and set every year on July 1. The rate is based on the 91-day Treasury bill rate + 1.70% during in-school periods, grace, and deferment periods, and based on the 91-day Treasury bill rate + 2.30% during repayment periods. The rates are capped at 8.25%. For the 2006-2007 academic year, the Stafford Loan rate is 6.8%.

Should the student become totally disabled or die, Stafford Loans are forgiven.

Perkins Loans are also part of the federal student aid program, but students cannot apply for them. These loans are administered by the college and are awarded based on federal guidelines for undergraduate and graduate students with "exceptional" financial need. The interest rate is fixed at 5%. Perkins Loans have a longer grace period than Stafford Loans. There are no fees associated with the Perkins Loan and it is capped at $4,000 annually.

Pell Grants and Federal Supplemental Educational Opportunity Grants (FSEOG) are also part of the federal Title IV program. These grants do not have to be repaid. However, they are designated for only the neediest of students. Both types of grantees are administered by colleges. Completion of the FAFSA is all that is necessary to apply for these two grants.

Academic Competitiveness Grant and National SMART Grant

In 2006, Congress created two more grant opportunities for very low income families. They are the Academic Competitiveness Grant (AC Grant) and the National Science and Mathematics Access to Retain Talent Grant (SMART Grant). Only students who qualify for a Pell Grant will be considered for these grants. The AC Grant, as defined on the United States Department of Education website (http://studentaid.ed.gov/PORTALSWebApp/students/english/AcademicGrants. jsp) follows:

"An eligible student may receive an Academic Competitiveness Grant (AC Grant) of up to $750 for the first academic year of study and up to $1,300 for the second academic year of study. To be eligible for each academic year, a student must:

- Be a U.S. citizen;

- Be a Federal Pell Grant recipient;

- Be enrolled full-time in a degree program;

- Be enrolled in the first or second academic year of his or her program of study at a two-year or four-year degree-granting institution;

- Have completed a rigorous secondary school program of study (after January 1, 2006, if a first-year student, and after January 1, 2005, if a second-year student);

- If a first-year student, not have previously enrolled in an under-graduate program; and

- If a second-year student, have at least a cumulative 3.0 grade point average on a 4.0 scale for the first academic year.

Note that the amount of the AC Grant, when combined with a Pell Grant, may not exceed the student's cost of attendance. In addition, if the number of eligible students is large enough that payment of the full grant amounts would exceed the program appropriation in any fiscal year, then the amount of the grant to each eligible student may be ratably reduced."

The SMART Grant as defined on the United States Department of Education website (http://studentaid.ed.gov/PORTALSWebApp/students/english/SmartGrants.jsp) follows:

"The National Science and Mathematics Access to Retain Talent Grant, also known as the National SMART Grant is available during the third and fourth years of undergraduate study to full-time students who are eligible for the Federal Pell Grant and who are majoring in physical, life, or computer sciences, mathematics, technology, or engineering or in a foreign language determined critical to national security. The student must also have maintained a cumulative grade point average (GPA) of at least 3.0 in coursework required for the major. The National SMART Grant award is in addition to the student's Pell Grant award."

"An eligible student may receive a National SMART Grant of up to $4,000 for each of the third and fourth academic years of study. To be eligible for each academic year, a student must:

- Be a U.S. citizen:

- Be a Federal Pell Grant recipient;

- Be enrolled full-time in a degree program;

- Be enrolled in a four-year degree granting institution;

- Major in physical, life or computer science, engineering, mathematics, technology, or a critical foreign language; and

- Have at least a cumulative 3.0 grade point average on a 4.0 scale (as set forth in regulations to be promulgated soon).

Note that the amount of the SMART Grant, when combined with a Pell Grant, may not exceed the student's cost of attendance. In addition, if the number of eligible students is large enough that payment of the full grant amounts would exceed the program appropriation in any fiscal year, the amount of the grant to each eligible student may be ratably reduced."

Alternative Student Loans

Students can also take alternative loans, sometimes called "signature loans." These loans are offered by private lenders and are not part of the federal loan program. The minimum loan is usually $500 and the maximum is the full cost of college minus any other financial aid the student is receiving. The interest rate is variable and based on the student's credit history. If the student has a cosigner, the cosigner's credit history may lower the rate. Fees associated with these loans will vary and should be investigated before taking the loan.

Parent Loans

Federal PLUS Loans (Parent Loans for Undergraduate Students) are for parents. These loans allow parents to borrow up to the full cost of college, minus any other financial aid the student is receiving. Features include the following:

- PLUS loans are not difficult to get. The application process is not as onerous as borrowing against your house. Parents simply need to demonstrate creditworthiness.

- Repayment begins within 60 days of the first disbursement, although parents can request deferment for up to 60 months while the student is in school.

- Depending on the lender, there may also be other beneficial repayment options similar to those of the federal student loans.

- The interest rate for new loans will change each year and is capped at 9%. For the 2006-2007 academic year, the rate is fixed at 8.5%.

- Repayment generally begins 60 days after the loan is disbursed. However parents can ask for a deferral of up to 60 months.

- Should the parent who signs the loan die or become totally disabled, the loan is forgiven.

Other Parent Loan Options

Unlike most students, many parents may have the option of using **home equity** to pay for college. In many instances, the interest rate may be tax deductible where the education loan interest deduction might not be available to parents who have higher incomes. (See "Student Loan Interest Deduction" under "Cash Flow Planning—Tax Benefits, below).

The funding can come from refinancing a mortgage to take cash out, or a home equity loan or line of credit. Should parents opt to borrow against the family home, however, advisors should review insurance needs to make sure they are protected against loss.

When evaluating the parent loan options, it may be necessary to do a spreadsheet to determine whether home equity is a better source of funds than federal PLUS loans. Loans against home equity, whether in the form of a line of credit or a mortgage refinance, will necessitate a look at the parent's existing debt burden as a part of their application process. So if it is likely that the parents will borrow from their home equity/mortgage as well as take out a PLUS loan, it might be advantageous to leave the PLUS loan until last so it doesn't affect the parents' ability to qualify for the home equity loan.

Federal Consolidation Loans

Although **Federal Consolidation Loans** are not a direct source of cash flow for paying college bills, they are a means of managing the debt. Federal Consolidation Loans allow parents and students to consolidate their loans into one loan with a new interest rate and repayment schedule. The rates for all loans being consolidated are averaged, and the borrower may have up to 30 years to repay. This repayment flexibility can result in a lower monthly payment; however, the total interest paid will naturally be higher than if the borrower opts for the typical 10-year repayment period.

State Loans and Grants

State loans and grants are also a source of cash flow for college. However it is beyond the scope this book to look at all 50 states. Suffice it to say that many states are eager to prevent the "brain drain" of students going to college out-of-state rather than staying in-state upon graduation. The states' strategy is to offer incentive loans and grants to residents who attend college in-state. Parents and students may wish to consider this source of college funding.

COLLEGE CASH FLOW TOOLS—TAX BENEFITS

Sooner or later, parents are going to have to figure out how to actually pay those college bills. If they have done their job right, they started saving when the baby was born and have plenty of savings already put aside. But no matter how diligent most parents are, many families will still come up short and have to deal with some cash flow issues. Uncle Sam has given us some tools to help with cash flow in the form of tax credits. They are the Hope Scholarship Credit and the Lifetime Learning Credit, as explained below:

- Both credits are available for qualified tuition and related expenses of a taxpayer, spouse, or dependent claimed on the taxpayer's return.

- A student cannot claim the credit if he is claimed as a dependent on his parent's return, even if the student paid the tuition.

- The credits cannot be claimed by a taxpayer who is married and filing separately.

- There are income phase-outs (indexed annually for inflation):

  - Married filing jointly, $94,000 - $114,000 (in 2007)

  - Single, Head of Household Qualifying Widow(er), $47,000 - $57,000 (in 2007)

- Qualifying expenses include tuition and fees, but not books and supplies (unless required to be purchased from the institution as part of enrollment), personal expenses, hobby courses, or fees that can be deducted elsewhere.

- Credits cannot be claimed for expenses that might be reimbursed, but are not taxed (e.g., a business-related course). If taxable, then the credit is allowed.

- A taxpayer cannot claim a Hope Scholarship Credit and Lifetime Learning Credit for the same student in the same year.

- Expenses covered by a scholarship cannot be included in the computation of the Hope Scholarship Credit or Lifetime Learning Credit.

- Expenses that are paid using a distribution from a Coverdell Education Savings Account or 529 Plan cannot be used to compute a Hope Scholarship Credit or Lifetime Learning Credit.

HOPE SCHOLARSHIP CREDIT

The Hope Scholarship Credit is available for use during the first two years of college only. It is a credit of 100% of the first $1,100 and 50% of the second $1,100 for each year, or a maximum of $1,650 per year (2007 tax year). This credit may be claimed per student, per year. The student must be enrolled in a degree or certificate program, be at least a half-time student, and must not have a felony drug conviction.

LIFETIME LEARNING CREDIT

The Lifetime Learning Credit is a credit of 20% of up to $10,000 of qualified tuition and fees during a tax year. It cannot exceed $2,000, and is not tied to a degree or certificate program. Unlike the Hope Scholarship Credit, there is no limit on the number of years the credit can be claimed for a student.

STUDENT LOAN INTEREST DEDUCTION

Congress has also given a break to students and parents who have to borrow to pay for college. This is an important feature because most federal financial aid—and state financial aid for that matter—is in the form of loans.

- Student loan interest is deductible in the year(s) loan payments are made up to $2,500.

- The interest cannot be deducted by an individual who is not legally responsible for payment of the loan, even if that person makes the payments (i.e., parents who make payments on their child's Stafford Loan or Perkins Loan cannot deduct the interest because they are not legally responsible for repaying the loan). Furthermore, if a student makes interest payments on his or her loan, but is claimed as a dependent on his or her parents' income tax return, the student cannot claim the deduction, nor can the parents.

- The deduction is not available to persons who are married and file separately.

- There are income phase-outs (indexed annually for inflation; for details, check IRS publication 970, Tax Benefits for Education):

  - Married, filing jointly: $110,000 - $140,000 (in 2007)

  - Single, Head of Household, Qualifying Widow(er): $55,000 - $70,000 (in 2007)

- The deduction must be coordinated with any nontaxable education benefits received (e.g., employer education assistance, nontaxable distributions from Coverdell Education Savings Accounts or 529 plans, Series EE or Series I savings bond interest exclusion, etc.).

FEDERAL TUITION DEDUCTION

For a brief period of time, federal income tax rules permits parents to take an income tax deduction for tuition paid. This deduction will expire after 2007. The deduction is limited by modified AGI, and there is no phase-out range.

Deduction Limit	Single, HOH, Qual. Widow(er)	Married filing jointly
$4,000	$0 - $65,000	$0 - $130,000
$2,000	$65,001 - $80,000	$130,001 - $160,000

Qualified education expenses are tuition and fees for the tax year in which they are paid. They must be reduced by (1) any tax-free educational assistance received (e.g., Pell Grants, scholarships, or employer-provided assistance), and (2) any expenses allocated to tax-free interest on United States savings bonds or tax-free distributions from a Coverdell Education Savings Account or 529 plan.

The deduction is not permitted in any years that a Hope Scholarship or Lifetime Learning Credit is claimed for the student, or any expenses are deducted under another provision of the law.

DIRECT TUITION PAYMENTS

Occasionally, a grandparent or other relative may want to make a gift to a college bound grandchild. Tuition payments made directly to a college or university on behalf of an individual for that's person's education or training (i.e., qualified transfers) are not considered to be taxable gifts. Note that such payments must be made *directly* to the college by the donor and cannot be gifted to the student or parent first. Moreover, care should be exercised if the student might also be receiving need-based financial aid. Colleges would view these gifts as an "outside resource" and would reduce the financial aid award accordingly. For more information, see Internal Revenue Service Publication 950 (Introduction to Estate and Gift Taxes), IRS Form 709 (United States Gift Tax Return) or 709-A (Instructions for Form 709). These documents are available on the IRS web site at www.IRS.gov in the Forms and Publications section, or by calling 1-800-TAX-FORM (1-800-829-3676).

Chapter 8

COLLEGE MONEY'S DIAGNOSTIC TOOLS

THE COLLEGE PLANNING CONVERSATION™

The College Planning Conversation™ (Figure 8.1) is a tool to help advisors (1) *quantify* parents' college goals, (2) *prompt* parents to commit to a preliminary college plan, and (3) *motivate* parents to accelerate action on their college plans based on how college will impact on their retirement. Once the initial conversation is completed, successive conversations can help tune and refine a plan.

The College Planning Conversation is based on an Excel® based spreadsheet program with a graphic interface. The spreadsheet portion shown can be used as a template for advisors to design their own custom illustrations for their clients. We added the graphics page to make it easier to motivate clients to take action.

Examples on how to use the College Planning Conversation can be found in Chapter 2 (the Sample case study) and in Chapter 3 (the Scott case study).

Important elements of this planning tool include:

- A college cost forecast showing the client his yearly cash flow on a bar graph as well as the total college bill for all children based on his education goals.

- A written summary of the client's commitment of resources to the college plan.

- A line graph showing the clients' college cash flow during the **savings period** (today through the start of college), the **spending and borrowing period** (the start of college through the end of college) and the **recovery period** (the end of college to the beginning of retirement).

Figure 8.1

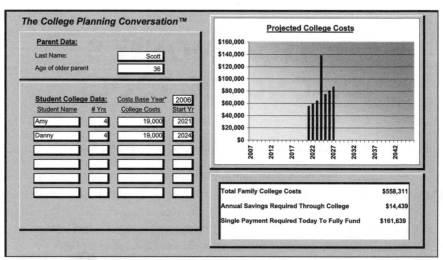

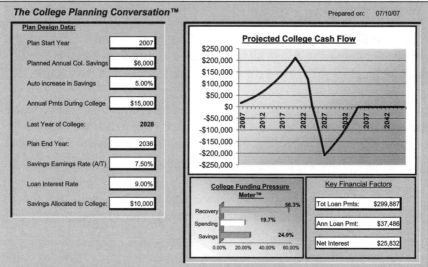

This program is designed to help plan future family college expenditures. Results are for planning purposes only and imply no guarantees. Program analysis is highly dependent on the accuracy of client input data. The validity of the college cost forecast requires annual updating of college cost and inflation data.

Version: 2007

*2006 – 2007

Figure 8.1 (Cont'd)

Prepared for: **Scott**

Subject: **College Funding Analysis**

The analysis that follows has been prepared especially for your family. The purpose of this analysis is to help you design a plan to handle anticipated future college costs in a reasonable and effective manner. You should understand the any analysis of this type is for planning purposes only. The projections imply guarantees. Projections are based on future college cost data, interest, and inflation assumptions, and personal data you supplied, all of which can change over time. used properly, however, this analysis can help you be better prepared to handle college for your family. For best results this analysis should be updated annually.

Parent Data:

Client name	Scott
Age of older parent	36
Plan end (year of older parent retirement or sooner	2036
Year first student starts college	2021
Year last student finishes college	2028
After-tax savings earnings rate	7.50%
Loan interest rate	9.00%
Savings already set aside for college	$10,000

Plan Design Data:

Planned annual college saving	$6,000
Planned annual increase in savings (percentage)	5.00%
Planned annual payments during college	$15,000

College Cost Database Used: 0

Student Data:

Student #	1	2	3	4	5	6
Student Name	Amy	Danny	0	0	0	0
College Start Year	2021	2024				
# Years in College	4	4	0	0	0	0
Last Year College	2025	2028				

Figure 8.1 (Cont'd)

COLLEGE COST FORECAST

The first step in developing a good college plan is to forecast what college is likely to cost for your family. The following table projects future college costs for each member of your family based on the current college cost you entered for each student.

@ 7.50% The single lump sum required today to fund college $161,639
@ 7.50% The annual savings required to fund college $14,439

Age Older Parent	Year	COLLEGE COSTS FOR STUDENT						TOTAL COSTS
		#1	#2	#3	#4	#5	#6	
36	2007	$0	$0	$0	$0	$0	$0	$0
37	2008	$0	$0	$0	$0	$0	$0	$0
38	2009	$0	$0	$0	$0	$0	$0	$0
39	2010	$0	$0	$0	$0	$0	$0	$0
40	2011	$0	$0	$0	$0	$0	$0	$0
41	2012	$0	$0	$0	$0	$0	$0	$0
42	2013	$0	$0	$0	$0	$0	$0	$0
43	2014	$0	$0	$0	$0	$0	$0	$0
44	2015	$0	$0	$0	$0	$0	$0	$0
45	2016	$0	$0	$0	$0	$0	$0	$0
46	2017	$0	$0	$0	$0	$0	$0	$0
47	2018	$0	$0	$0	$0	$0	$0	$0
48	2019	$0	$0	$0	$0	$0	$0	$0
49	2020	$0	$0	$0	$0	$0	$0	$0
50	2021	$54,980	$0	$0	$0	$0	$0	$54,980
51	2022	$59,329	$0	$0	$0	$0	$0	$59,329
52	2023	$64,022	$0	$0	$0	$0	$0	$64,022
53	2024	$69,086	$69,086	$0	$0	$0	$0	$138,172
54	2025	$0	$74,551	$0	$0	$0	$0	$74,551
55	2026	$0	$80,447	$0	$0	$0	$0	$80,447
56	2027	$0	$86,811	$0	$0	$0	$0	$86,811
57	2028	$0	$0	$0	$0	$0	$0	$0
58	2029	$0	$0	$0	$0	$0	$0	$0
59	2030	$0	$0	$0	$0	$0	$0	$0
60	2031	$0	$0	$0	$0	$0	$0	$0
61	2032	$0	$0	$0	$0	$0	$0	$0
62	2033	$0	$0	$0	$0	$0	$0	$0
63	2034	$0	$0	$0	$0	$0	$0	$0
64	2035	$0	$0	$0	$0	$0	$0	$0
65	2036	$0	$0	$0	$0	$0	$0	$0
66	2037	$0	$0	$0	$0	$0	$0	$0
67	2038	$0	$0	$0	$0	$0	$0	$0
68	2039	$0	$0	$0	$0	$0	$0	$0
69	2040	$0	$0	$0	$0	$0	$0	$0
70	2041	$0	$0	$0	$0	$0	$0	$0
71	2042	$0	$0	$0	$0	$0	$0	$0
72	2043	$0	$0	$0	$0	$0	$0	$0
73	2044	$0	$0	$0	$0	$0	$0	$0
74	2045	$0	$0	$0	$0	$0	$0	$0
75	2046	$0	$0	$0	$0	$0	$0	$0
TOTALS		$247,416	$310,895	$0	$0	$0	$0	$558,311

Figure 8.1 (Cont'd)

A Composite College Funding Plan for:	Scott		10-Jul-07
1. Add new savings to your college funding account this year in the amount of			$6,000
2. Increase college savings each year until college starts at the rate of			5.00%
3. Once college starts make transfers from current income each year of			$15,000
4. Borrow the balance and repay loans prior to retirement @ interest of		9.00%	$37,486
5. Invest net proceeds @ an interest rate of		7.50%	

Age of Older Parent	Year	Total College Costs 0	Save $10,000	Transfer	Loan Pmts	Net Interest	Acct Bal
36	2007	$0	$6,000	$0			$16,000
37	2008	$0	$6,300	$0	$0	$1,200	$23,500
38	2009	$0	$6,615	$0	$0	$1,763	$31,878
39	2010	$0	$6,946	$0	$0	$2,391	$41,214
40	2011	$0	$7,293	$0	$0	$3,091	$51,598
41	2012	$0	$7,658	$0	$0	$3,870	$63,126
42	2013	$0	$8,041	$0	$0	$4,734	$75,901
43	2014	$0	$8,443	$0	$0	$5,693	$90,036
44	2015	$0	$8,865	$0	$0	$6,753	$105,653
45	2016	$0	$9,308	$0	$0	$7,924	$122,885
46	2017	$0	$9,773	$0	$0	$9,216	$141,875
47	2018	$0	$10,262	$0	$0	$10,641	$162,778
48	2019	$0	$10,775	$0	$0	$12,208	$185,761
49	2020	$0	$11,314	$0	$0	$13,932	$211,007
50	2021	$54,980	$0	$15,000	$0	$15,826	$186,853
51	2022	$59,329	$0	$15,000	$0	$14,014	$156,538
52	2023	$64,022	$0	$15,000	$0	$11,740	$119,257
53	2024	$138,172	$0	$15,000	$0	$8,944	$5,029
54	2025	$74,551	$0	$15,000	$0	$377	-$54,144
55	2026	$80,447	$0	$15,000	$0	-$4,873	-$124,465
56	2027	$86,811	$0	$15,000	$0	-$11,202	-$207,477
57	2028	$0	$0	$0	$37,486	-$18,673	-$188,665
58	2029	$0	$0	$0	$37,486	-$16,980	-$168,158
59	2030	$0	$0	$0	$37,486	-$15,134	-$145,807
60	2031	$0	$0	$0	$37,486	-$13,123	-$121,444
61	2032	$0	$0	$0	$37,486	-$10,930	-$94,888
62	2033	$0	$0	$0	$37,486	-$8,540	-$65,942
63	2034	$0	$0	$0	$37,486	-$5,935	-$34,391
64	2035	$0	$0	$0	$37,486	-$3,095	$0
65	2036	$0	$0	$0	$0	$0	$0
66	2037	$0	$0	$0	$0	$0	$0
67	2038	$0	$0	$0	$0	$0	$0
68	2039	$0	$0	$0	$0	$0	$0
69	2040	$0	$0	$0	$0	$0	$0
70	2041	$0	$0	$0	$0	$0	$0
71	2042	$0	$0	$0	$0	$0	$0
72	2043	$0	$0	$0	$0	$0	$0
73	2044	$0	$0	$0	$0	$0	$0
74	2045	$0	$0	$0	$0	$0	$0
75	2046	$0	$0	$0	$0	$0	$0
TOTALS		$558,311	$127,592	$105,000	$299,887	$25,832	n/a

HOW TO PLAN for College

Figure 8.1 (Cont'd)

Prepared For: **Scott**

Prepared On: 10-Jul-07

Subject: **Planning Recommendations:**

1 Begin a savings plan as quickly as possible.

You don't have to save everything right now. Saving even small amounts is more important than not saving. Early savings enjoy the benefit of compound growth. This means that every dollar you save now will result in more than a dollar that won't have to be borrowed later.

2 Make sure that your savings plan considers the following key features:

a. Your plan should avoid the "Kiddie Tax."
b. Your plan should allow for controlled taxation of savings growth.
c. Your plan should allow for controlled taxation during the withdrawal phase.
d. Your plan should provide flexibility to deal with future financial aid eligibility.
e. Your plan should allow multiple investment options that consider:
  - Staying ahead of college inflation rates.
  - Diversifying your risk.
  - Making changes at reasonable cost both as markets change and as your needs change, particularly as you get close to the withdrawal phase.
f. Your plan should consider self completion in the event of the death or disability of all breadwinners.
g. Your plan should consider a "pay yourself first" option that allows automatic, systematic plan deposits.

3 Complete a Financial Aid Test™ now.

The Financial Aid Test™ can help you to assess your potential future eligibility for financial aid. Knowing your likelihood of qualifying for future financial aid will help you judge the desirability of implementing "pay-as-you-go" or other strategies during the college years.

4 Review your retirement plans, now.

College is part of the retirement problem. Without proper thought, you are likely to invade retirement funds to pay for college or are likely to over borrow for college and be caught repaying college loans at a time you should be saving for your own retirement.

5 Review your plan at least annually.

THE FINANCIAL AID TEST™

The Financial Aid Test™ (Figure 8.2) is a diagnostic tool that calculates the Parent Expected Contribution (PEC), the Student Expected Contribution (SEC), and the Family Expected Contribution (FEC) under the Federal Methodology and the Institutional Methodology. It can be used in several ways:

- First, when developing a long-term college savings plan, the Financial Aid Test can examine the likelihood of a student qualifying for financial aid. It should be used in conjunction with the Financial Aid Appraisal™ in order to develop a complete picture. This combination can be helpful in the design phase so that appropriate products and account titles are used (see, e.g., the Scott case study in this chapter).

- Second, in developing a crisis college plan, the Financial Aid Test can be used to help identify a planning category and its appropriate planning strategy (see, e.g., the Dillon case study in this chapter).

- Third, in a crisis plan in conjunction with the Financial Aid Appraisal™, the Financial Aid Test can help develop a college cash flow plan (see, e.g., the Dillon case study in this chapter).

- Fourth, in a crisis planning case, the Financial Aid Test can be used to confirm or challenge a financial aid award (see, e.g., the Dillon case in this chapter).

- Finally, as a prospecting tool, the Financial Aid Test can act as a filter when used in a college planning workshop to choose appropriate clients (see *The College Planning Presentation Study Guide*).

Figure 8.2 is an Excel® based spreadsheet program with a graphic interface. We added the graphics page to make it easier to motivate clients to take action. Important elements of the Financial Aid Test include:

- The Parent Expected Contribution (PEC), the Student Expected Contribution (SEC), and the Family Expected Contribution (FEC) under the *Federal* Methodology

- The Parent Expected Contribution (PEC), the Student Expected Contribution (SEC), and the Family Expected Contribution (FEC) under the *Institutional* Methodology

Figure 8.2

The Financial Aid Test™

Version 2007
11-Jul-07

Family Data:

Parent's Name (in report form)	Scott
Student's Name (in report form)	Amy
Street Address	9876 Main Street
City, State, ZIP	Passaic, NJ 01234
Home Telephone:	610-000-0000
Business Telephone:	215-000-0000
State of Residence (All Caps, e.g., NJ)	NJ
1 Age of Older Parent	36
2 Number of Parents in Family	2
3 Number of Dependent Children in Family	2
4 Number of Students in College for Plan Year	1
5 Total Ages of All Pre-college Children	1

Student Financial Data:

23 Student's Assets	$0
24 Student's Income	
a From Work	$0
b From Investments	$0
25 Student Income Tax Paid	$0
26 Assets in Siblings Names (IM only)	$0

Parent Financial Data:

6	Father's Wages	$99,000
7	Mother's Wages	$20,000
8	Other Taxable Income	$500
9	Nontaxable income	$0
10	Untaxed Benefits	$0
11	Losses from Business, Farm, Capital Losse	$0
12	Adjustments to Income	$0
13	Child Support Paid	$0
14	Tuition Tax Credits	$0
15	Taxable Student Aid	$0
16	Medical & Dental Expense	$3,500
17	Federal Income Taxes Paid	$8,000
18	Net Home Equity (include farm if you live on it)	
	a Market Value	$300,000
	b Sum of All Mortgages	$220,000
19	Net Equity of Other Real Estate	
	a Market Value	$0
	b Sum of All Mortgages	$0
20	Business/Farm Net Value (Your Share)	
	a Business Net Value	$0
	b Farm Net Value (if not used as residence)	$0
21	Parent Cash	$3,000
22	Parent Investments	
	a Qualified Retirement Plans	$143,500
	b Other	$10,000
	Debts other than mortgages	$0

The Financial Aid Test™ - Quick Calc

Federal Methodology

Parent Expected Cont./Student	$26,584
Student Expected Contribution	$0
Expected Family Contribution/Student	$26,584

Key Counseling Numbers
Federal Methodology

	Assets	Income
% EPC From:	0.00%	100.00%
% ESC From:	0.00%	0.00%
Par. Marg.Cont.:	5.64%	47.00%
Stud. Marg. Cont:	20.00%	50.00%

Institutional Methodology

Parent Expected Cont./Student	$21,377
Student Expected Contribution	$1,550
Expected Family Contribution/Student	$22,927

Key Counseling Numbers
Institutional Methodology

	Assets	Income
% EPC From:	7.31%	92.69%
% ESC From:	0.00%	100.00%
Par. Marg. Cont:	4.00%	46.00%
Stud. Marg. Cont:	25.00%	50.00%

This analysis provides estimated financial aid data for planning purposes only. Actual financial aid awards are determined by each college at the time of admission. The validity of the input data can dramatically affect financial aid values. Which assets must be counted and how each asset is valued may be treated differently by the government and each individual college. Calculations are based on

Federal Methodology	2007-08
Institutional Methodology	2007-08

Source: "CSS/Financial Aid PROFILE® User's Guide"

Figure 8.2 (Cont'd)

Counselor Worksheet   Version 2007

The Financial Aid Test - Data Verification   11-Jul-07

Parent's name	Scott
Student's name	Amy
Address	9876 Main Street
City, state, zip	Passaic, NJ 01234
Home telephone	610-000-0000
Business telephone	215-000-0000

1 Age of older parent	36
2 Number of parents in family	2
3 No. of dependent children in the family	2
4 Number of students in college (planned)	1
5 Total ages of all pre-college children	1
6 Father's wages	$99,000
7 Mother's wages	$20,000
8 Other taxable income	$500
9 Untaxed benefits	$0
10 Losses from business, farm, capital losses)	$0
11 Non-taxable income	$0
12 Child support paid	$0
13 Tuition tax credits	$0
14 Taxable student aid	$0
15 Medical & dental expense	$3,500
16 Adjustments to income	$0
17 Federal income tax paid	$8,000
18 Net home equity	
a Market value	$300,000
b Sum of all mortgages	$220,000
19 Net equity of other real estate	
a Market value	$0
b Sum of all mortgages	$0
20 Business/farm net value (your share)	$0
21 Parent cash	$3,000
22 Parent investments	
a Qualified retirement plans	$143,500
b Other	$10,000
Other debt	$0
23 Student assets	$0
24 Student income	
a From work	$0
b From investments	$0
25 Student income tax paid	$0
26 Assets in siblings names (IM only)	$0
State code New Jersey NJ	

Figure 8.2 (Cont'd)

Parent's name:	Scott
Student's name:	Amy
Prepared on:	11-Jul-07

Parent Expected Contribution - Calculations		Federal	Institutional
Parent's income			
Father's income from work		$99,000	$99,000
Mother's income from work		$20,000	$20,000
Other taxable income		$500	$500
Non-taxable income		$0	$0
Untaxed benefits		$0	$0
Losses from business, farm, capital losses (add back)		n/a	$0
Total income		$119,500	$119,500
Income Exclusions			
Child support paid		$0	$0
Tuition tax credits		$0	n/a
Taxable Student aid		$0	n/a
Total income exclusions		$0	$0
Total income less exclusions		$119,500	$119,500
Deductions:			
FICA tax - father		$7,276	$7,276
FICA tax - mother		$1,530	$1,530
Total FICA tax		$8,806	$8,806
Adjustments to income		$0	$0
U.S. income tax paid		$8,000	$8,000
State & other taxes		$8,365	$12,548
Employment expense allowance		$3,200	$3,970
Medical & dental allowance		n/a	$0
Annual Education Savings Allowance	$1,816	n/a	$1,816
Income protection allowance		$23,070	$26,090
Total deductions		$51,441	$61,230
Available income (AI)		$68,059	$58,270
Total Parent Contribution from Income (IM only)	46.00%	n/a	$19,814

Figure 8.2 (Cont'd)

Counselor Worksheet
The Financial Aid Test
Federal & Institutional Methodologies for: 2007-08

Parent's name:	Scott		
Student's name:	Amy		
Prepared on:	11-Jul-07		

Parent's assets			
Parent cash		$3,000	$3,000
Home equity (IM only)		n/a	$80,000
Market value	$300,000		
Mortgage value	$220,000		
Other real estate equity		$0	$0
Market value	$0		
Mortgage value	$0		
Parent investments (excl ret plans)		$10,000	$10,000
Business/farm net worth	$0	$0	$0
Assets in siblings names (IM only)		n/a	$0
Net worth		$13,000	$93,000
Asset protection allowance (FM only)		$27,900	n/a
Emergency reserve allowance (IM only)		n/a	$24,260
Cummulative educ savings allowance (IM only)		n/a	$22,251
Low income allowance (IM only)		n/a	$0
Total asset allowances		$27,900	$46,511
Discretionary net worth (DNW)		$0	$46,489
Asset conversion rate		12.00%	4.00%
Income supplement (FM only)		$0	n/a
Total parent contribution from assets (IM only)		n/a	$1,564
Adjusted available income (AAI)		$68,059	n/a
AAI contribution rate		47.00%	n/a
Total contribution from income (IM only)		n/a	$19,814
Total parent's contribution	$26,584	$26,584	$21,377
Number of students in college		1	1
Number in college adjustment			100.00%
Parent's Contribution Per Student		**$26,584**	**$21,377**

Figure 8.2 (Cont'd)

Counselor Worksheet   **Page 4**
The Financial Aid Test   **Version 2007**
Federal & Institutional Methodologies for: 2007-08

Parent's name:	Scott	
Student's name:	Amy	
Prepared on:	11-Jul-07	

Dependent Student Contribution:	Federal	Institutional
Student income		
Student's earned income	$0	$0
Student's other income	$0	$0
Student's total income	$0	$0
Student's deductions		
U.S. income tax paid	$0	$0
FICA tax paid	$0	$0
State & other taxes	$0	$0
Income protection allowance	$3,000	n/a
Parent negative AI Offset	$0	n/a
Total deductions	$3,000	$0
Net student income	-$3,000	$0
Income assessment rate	50.00%	50.00%
Available income	$0	$1,550
Student's assets	$0	$0
Conversion rate	20.00%	25.00%
Income supplement	$0	$0
Student Contribution	**$0**	**$1,550**
TOTAL FAMILY CONTRIBUTION	**$26,584**	**$22,927**

Figure 8.2 (Cont'd)

Counselor Worksheet   Page 5
The Financial Aid Test   Version 2007
Federal & Institutional Methodologies for: 2007-08

KEY COUNSELING NUMBERS **Federal Methodology**	Totals	% From Assets	% From Income
Total Parent Expected Cont.	$26,584		
Parent Expected Cont./Student	$26,584	0.00%	100.00%
Student Expected Contribution	$0	0.00%	0.00%
Family Expected Cont. This Student	$26,584		
Parent Asset Gap	$14,900		
Student Income Gap	$3,000		

FINANCIAL AID PLANNING RULES OF THUMB **Federal Methodology**		% From Assets	% From Income
Parent's Marginal Contribution Percentage		5.64%	47.00%
Student's Marginal Contribution Percentage		20.00%	50.00%

KEY COUNSELING NUMBERS **Institutional Methodology**	Totals	% From Assets	% From Income
Total Parent Expected Cont. (Formula)	$21,377	7.31%	92.69%
Parent Expected Cont. This Student 100.00%	$21,377		
Student Expected Contribution	$1,550	0.00%	100.00%
Family Expected Cont. This Student	$22,927		
Parent Asset Gap	$0		
Student Income Gap	$0		

FINANCIAL AID PLANNING RULES OF THUMB **Institutional Methodology**		% From Assets	% From Income
Parent's Marginal Contribution Percentage		4.00%	46.00%
Student's Marginal Contribution Percentage		25.00%	50.00%

Figure 8.2 (Cont'd)

The Financial Aid Test™   Version 2007

| Prepared for: | Scott |
| And Student: | Amy |

INPUT DATA VERIFICATION SUMMARY AS OF: 11-Jul-07

1 Age of older parent	36
2 Number of parents in family	2
3 No. of dependent children in the family	2
4 Number of students in college (planned)	1
5 Total ages of all pre-college children	1
6 Father's wages	$99,000
7 Mother's wages	$20,000
8 Other taxable income	$500
9 Untaxed benefits	$0
10 Losses from business, farm, capital losses	$0
11 Non taxable income	$0
12 Child Support Paid	$0
13 Tuition tax credits	$0
14 Taxable student aid	$0
15 Medical & dental expense	$3,500
16 Adjustments to income	$0
17 Federal income tax paid	$8,000
18 Net home equity (not used in Federal Methodology)	$80,000
19 Net equity of other real estate	$0
20 Business net value (your share)	$0
21 Parent cash	$3,000
22 Parent investments (non retirement)	$10,000
23 Student assets	$0
24 Student income	$0
a From work	$0
b From investments	
25 Student income tax paid	$0
26 Assets in siblings' names (not used in Federal Methodology)	$0
State code	NJ

FAMILY EXPECTED CONTRIBUTION SUMMARY:	Federal	Institutional
Parent Contribution Per Student	**$26,584**	**$21,377**
Student Contribution	**$0**	**$1,550**
FAMILY CONTRIBUTION THIS STUDENT:	**$26,584**	**$22,927**

This analysis provides estimated financial aid data for planning purposes only. Actual financial aid awards are determined by each college at the time of admission. The validity of the input data can dramatically affect financial aid values. Which assets must be counted and how each asset is valued may be treated differently by the government and each individual college. Calculations are based on:

| Federal Methodology | 2007-08 |
| Institutional Methodology | 2007-08 |

- Key counseling numbers that can be used to help reduce the expected contributions in crisis planning mode

Advisors can use other financial aid calculators available on the web, such as the one found on the College Board web site at: http://apps.collegeboard.com/fincalc/ efc_welcome.jsp.

THE FINANCIAL AID APPRAISAL™

The purpose of the Financial Aid Appraisal™ (Figure 8.3) is to project potential financial aid into the future. When planning early for college it is important to investigate whether or not financial aid might help with future college costs. The process involves using the Financial Aid Test at the beginning of the planning process and calculating the Parent Expected Contribution (PEC) as though the student were going to attend college at that time. The Financial Aid Appraisal™ takes the PEC value and applies an inflation rate as well as potential changes that the family visualizes in their financial circumstances. The result is a forecast of potential future financial aid.

If the financial aid forecast indicates substantial aid is possible, appropriate planning tools should be used (see, e.g., the Chuck and Ann Sample case in Chapter 2).

Caution: If financial aid is possible, ongoing monitoring of the family financial circumstances and changes in the financial aid rules is critical to make sure that the family does not rely on financial aid that may no longer be forthcoming.

The Financial Aid Appraisal is an Excel® based spreadsheet with a graphic interface. The spreadsheet in Figure 8.3 can serve as a template for advisors who wish to design a custom illustration for their clients. The graphic interface was added to help motivate clients to take action.

Although actual financial aid packages are calculated using the Family Expected Contribution (FEC), the appropriate number to use here is the Parent Expected Contribution (PEC). We're attempting to calculate what the parent will need to pay. We also assume that if financial aid is a future possibility, then part of the planning process will be to attempt to minimize the student's contribution. Other examples of how the Financial Aid Appraisal is used can be found in this chapter (see the Scott case study).

Figure 8.3

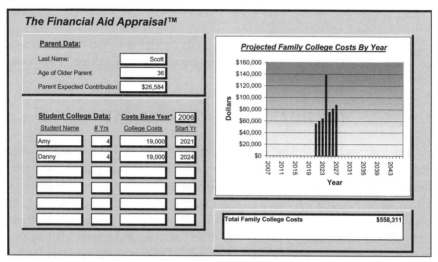

The Financial Aid Appraisal™

Parent Data:

Last Name:	Scott
Age of Older Parent	36
Parent Expected Contribution	$26,584

Student College Data: | **Costs Base Year*** 2006

Student Name	# Yrs	College Costs	Start Yr
Amy	4	19,000	2021
Danny	4	19,000	2024

Projected Family College Costs By Year

Total Family College Costs	$558,311

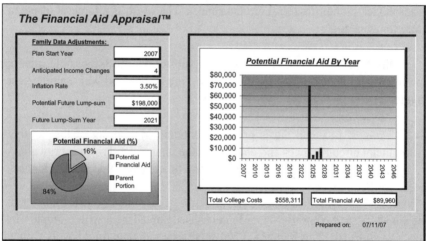

The Financial Aid Appraisal™

Family Data Adjustments:

Plan Start Year	2007
Anticipated Income Changes	4
Inflation Rate	3.50%
Potential Future Lump-sum	$198,000
Future Lump-Sum Year	2021

Potential Financial Aid (%)

- 16% Potential Financial Aid
- 84% Parent Portion

Potential Financial Aid By Year

Total College Costs	$558,311		Total Financial Aid	$89,960

Prepared on: 07/11/07

This program is designed to help families plan for future college expenditures. It projects future college costs and future financial aid eligibility based on current and past college cost data and current financial aid formulas which can change substantially over time. **This program is intended for planning purposes only and implies no guarantees.**

Projecting college costs and financial aid can be useful in the planning process to help decide on savings commitments and college funding vehicles. But for best results, projections should be recalculated annually using the most current version of this spreadsheet.

Version: 2007

*2006 – 2007

Figure 8.3 (Cont'd)

Prepared for: **Scott**

Subject: **The Financial Aid Appraisal™**

This analysis has been prepared especially for your family. Its purpose is to help you design a plan to handle anticipated future college costs and potential future financial aid in a reasonable and effective manner. It enables you to decide whether potential future financial aid would benefit you more than tax savings.

You should understand that any analysis of this type is for planning purposes only. **The projections imply no guarantees.**

Projections are based on future college cost data, interest, and inflation assumptions, and personal data you supplied, all of which can change over time. Financial aid projections assume current financial aid rules, which can change over time.

If used properly, however, this analysis can help you be better prepared to handle college for your family. **For best results this analysis should be updated annually.**

Figure 8.3 (Cont'd)

College Cost Forecast

The first step in developing a good college plan is to forecast what college is likely to cost for your family. The following table projects future college costs for each member of your family based on college costs you entered.

Age Older Parent	Year	COLLEGE COSTS FOR STUDENT #1	#2	#3	#4	#5	#6	TOTAL COSTS
36	2007	$0	$0	$0	$0	$0	$0	$0
37	2008	$0	$0	$0	$0	$0	$0	$0
38	2009	$0	$0	$0	$0	$0	$0	$0
39	2010	$0	$0	$0	$0	$0	$0	$0
40	2011	$0	$0	$0	$0	$0	$0	$0
41	2012	$0	$0	$0	$0	$0	$0	$0
42	2013	$0	$0	$0	$0	$0	$0	$0
43	2014	$0	$0	$0	$0	$0	$0	$0
44	2015	$0	$0	$0	$0	$0	$0	$0
45	2016	$0	$0	$0	$0	$0	$0	$0
46	2017	$0	$0	$0	$0	$0	$0	$0
47	2018	$0	$0	$0	$0	$0	$0	$0
48	2019	$0	$0	$0	$0	$0	$0	$0
49	2020	$0	$0	$0	$0	$0	$0	$0
50	2021	$54,980	$0	$0	$0	$0	$0	$54,980
51	2022	$59,329	$0	$0	$0	$0	$0	$59,329
52	2023	$64,022	$0	$0	$0	$0	$0	$64,022
53	2024	$69,086	$69,086	$0	$0	$0	$0	$138,172
54	2025	$0	$74,551	$0	$0	$0	$0	$74,551
55	2026	$0	$80,447	$0	$0	$0	$0	$80,447
56	2027	$0	$86,811	$0	$0	$0	$0	$86,811
57	2028	$0	$0	$0	$0	$0	$0	$0
58	2029	$0	$0	$0	$0	$0	$0	$0
59	2030	$0	$0	$0	$0	$0	$0	$0
60	2031	$0	$0	$0	$0	$0	$0	$0
61	2032	$0	$0	$0	$0	$0	$0	$0
62	2033	$0	$0	$0	$0	$0	$0	$0
63	2034	$0	$0	$0	$0	$0	$0	$0
64	2035	$0	$0	$0	$0	$0	$0	$0
65	2036	$0	$0	$0	$0	$0	$0	$0
66	2037	$0	$0	$0	$0	$0	$0	$0
67	2038	$0	$0	$0	$0	$0	$0	$0
68	2039	$0	$0	$0	$0	$0	$0	$0
69	2040	$0	$0	$0	$0	$0	$0	$0
70	2041	$0	$0	$0	$0	$0	$0	$0
71	2042	$0	$0	$0	$0	$0	$0	$0
72	2043	$0	$0	$0	$0	$0	$0	$0
73	2044	$0	$0	$0	$0	$0	$0	$0
74	2045	$0	$0	$0	$0	$0	$0	$0
75	2046	$0	$0	$0	$0	$0	$0	$0
TOTALS		$247,416	$310,895	$0	$0	$0	$0	$558,311

Figure 8.3 (Cont'd)

Potential Financial Aid

The potential financial aid calculation begins with an estimate of your Parent Expected Contribution (PEC calculated as though your student would attend college next year. It uses the current financial aid formulas and your current financial data. This estimated PEC is calculated using The Financial Aid Test™ software and is input into this program. The PEC is inflated using a PEC multiplier, which takes into account your feelings regarding your family's income and asset growth rates. Potential financial aid is an estimate for planning purposes only and is not a guarantee of financial aid.

Age Older Parent	Year	Total Costs	PEC Multiplier	Projected PEC	PEC from Lump-sum	Total Proj PEC	Potential Fin Aid
36	2007	$0	4.55%	$26,584	$0	$26,584	$0
37	2008	$0	4.55%	$27,794	$0	$27,794	$0
38	2009	$0	4.55%	$29,058	$0	$29,058	$0
39	2010	$0	4.55%	$30,380	$0	$30,380	$0
40	2011	$0	4.55%	$31,763	$0	$31,763	$0
41	2012	$0	4.55%	$33,208	$0	$33,208	$0
42	2013	$0	4.55%	$34,719	$0	$34,719	$0
43	2014	$0	4.55%	$36,298	$0	$36,298	$0
44	2015	$0	4.55%	$37,950	$0	$37,950	$0
45	2016	$0	4.55%	$39,677	$0	$39,677	$0
46	2017	$0	4.55%	$41,482	$0	$41,482	$0
47	2018	$0	4.55%	$43,370	$0	$43,370	$0
48	2019	$0	4.55%	$45,343	$0	$45,343	$0
49	2020	$0	4.55%	$47,406	$0	$47,406	$0
50	2021	$54,980	4.55%	$49,563	$11,880	$61,443	$0
51	2022	$59,329	4.55%	$51,818	$11,880	$63,698	$0
52	2023	$64,022	4.55%	$54,176	$11,880	$66,056	$0
53	2024	$138,172	4.55%	$56,641	$11,880	$68,521	$69,651
54	2025	$74,551	4.55%	$59,218	$11,880	$71,098	$3,453
55	2026	$80,447	4.55%	$61,912	$11,880	$73,792	$6,655
56	2027	$86,811	4.55%	$64,729	$11,880	$76,609	$10,202
57	2028	$0	4.55%	$67,675	$11,880	$79,555	$0
58	2029	$0	4.55%	$70,754	$11,880	$82,634	$0
59	2030	$0	4.55%	$73,973	$11,880	$85,853	$0
60	2031	$0	4.55%	$77,339	$11,880	$89,219	$0
61	2032	$0	4.55%	$80,858	$11,880	$92,738	$0
62	2033	$0	4.55%	$84,537	$11,880	$96,417	$0
63	2034	$0	4.55%	$88,383	$11,880	$100,263	$0
64	2035	$0	4.55%	$92,405	$11,880	$104,285	$0
65	2036	$0	4.55%	$96,609	$11,880	$108,489	$0
66	2037	$0	4.55%	$101,005	$11,880	$112,885	$0
67	2038	$0	4.55%	$105,600	$11,880	$117,480	$0
68	2039	$0	4.55%	$110,405	$11,880	$122,285	$0
69	2040	$0	4.55%	$115,429	$11,880	$127,309	$0
70	2041	$0	4.55%	$120,681	$11,880	$132,561	$0
71	2042	$0	4.55%	$126,172	$11,880	$138,052	$0
72	2043	$0	4.55%	$131,912	$11,880	$143,792	$0
73	2044	$0	4.55%	$137,914	$11,880	$149,794	$0
74	2045	$0	4.55%	$144,190	$11,880	$156,070	$0
75	2046	$0	4.55%	$150,750	$11,880	$162,630	$0
TOTALS		$558,311					**$89,960**

Important elements of the Financial Aid Appraisal include:

- A bar graph showing the estimated cost of college for each year of expected student enrollment.

- A summary of anticipated changes to the family's financial circumstances.

- A bar graph showing estimated financial aid during each year of expected enrollment.

- A pie chart showing the impact that estimated potential financial aid can have on the total family college bill.

THE FAMILY SCHOLARSHIP PLAN™

The Family Scholarship Plan™ (Figure 8.4) is a strategy, not a product. It has three main functions:

1. to *focus* the college planning client's attention on the benefits that a carefully crafted college plan can produce (instead of focusing on the product);

2. to *get* the client to recognize that different plan beneficiaries may have different needs and, therefore, require different products or tools in their savings plan; and

3. to *communicate* the college plan to other family members, such as grandparents, aunts, and uncles, who might be motivated to contribute to the college plan.

The Family Scholarship Plan is a graphic (Figure 8.4) that can be shown to a client during the diagnostic phase of college planning. Examples of how to use The Family Scholarship Plan can be found in Chapter 2 (see the Chuck and Ann Sample case study) and in this chapter (see the Scott case study).

Important components of this tool include:

- The *advisor toolbox* listing financial vehicles typically used in creating college planning solutions. Seeing this list of tools can prepare a client to expect that some of these tools will be recommended for his plan. Since the tools will be used only if they offer benefits that the client has identified as desirable, and that those benefits outweigh the costs and any disadvantages associated with the tool, negative connotations associated with the tool can be overcome.

- The *client benefits box* offers a list of benefits that college planning tools typically offer. Once the client understands that these benefits will be incorporated into his college plan if possible, he is more likely to implement the plan.

Figure 8.4 Family Scholarship Plan

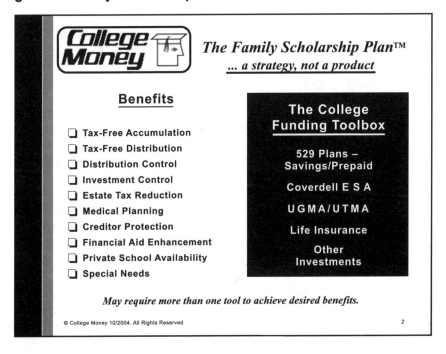

The Family Scholarship Plan™
... a strategy, not a product

Benefits

☐ Tax-Free Accumulation
☐ Tax-Free Distribution
☐ Distribution Control
☐ Investment Control
☐ Estate Tax Reduction
☐ Medical Planning
☐ Creditor Protection
☐ Financial Aid Enhancement
☐ Private School Availability
☐ Special Needs

The College Funding Toolbox

529 Plans –
Savings/Prepaid

Coverdell E S A

U G M A / U T M A

Life Insurance

Other
Investments

May require more than one tool to achieve desired benefits.

© College Money 10/2004. All Rights Reserved   2

THE BENEFIT EVALUATION FORM™

The Benefit Evaluation Form™ (Figure 8.5) is an adjunct to the Family Scholarship Plan graphic. Its function is to allow an advisor to record any client feelings regarding potential benefits of the Family Scholarship Plan. The advisor can evaluate and prioritize his or her value to the client. This tool can then be used in conjunction with the Tool/Benefits Grid™ in order to choose the appropriate tools. Examples on how to use the Benefit Evaluation Form can be found in the Scott case study in this chapter.

Figure 8.5

Benefits Evaluation Form™ The Family Scholarship Plan™	Ranking 10 = Most Important 1 = Least Important
1 Tax-free growth	
2 Tax-free distributions	
3 Investment control	
4 Distribution control	
5 Estate planning	
6 Creditor protection	
7 Medical planning	
8 Ability to pay for private elementary and secondary school	
9 Financial aid availability	
10 Ability to fund for special needs	

THE FAMILY BENEFIT CONSOLIDATION SUMMARY™

The Family Benefit Consolidation Summary (Figure 8.6) is a tool is used in grandparent-initiated college savings plans, both long-term and crisis. Grandparents need to plan separately for each student for: (1) the differing needs of the grandchildren; (2) crisis planning when need-based aid is likely and when it is not likely; and (3) long-term savings when need-based financial aid is likely and not likely.

The purpose of this process is to assist grandparents in planning by creating a side-by-side illustration of the benefits desired by both parties. This side-by-side comparison creates the ability to give appropriate weight to the necessary benefits and appropriate tools when building a plan.

THE TOOL/BENEFITS GRID™

The Tool/Benefits Grid™ (Figure 8.7) is a table listing some typical college planning tools and their benefits. This tool is used in conjunction with the Family Scholarship Plan™ and the Benefit Evaluation Form™ to choose the right tools to implement in a college plan. Examples of the grid can be found in the Scott case study (discussed in this chapter).

The Tool/Benefit Grid is by nature somewhat subjective. It is not meant to be precise. It is only a guide to be used with the advisor's knowledge, experience, and his evaluation of the client's needs in choosing the correct tools.

Figure 8.6

Family Benefit Consolidation Summary™		
	Grandparent Data	**Student Data**
Planning Status (crisis or long-term savings)		
Tax-free growth		
Tax-free distributions		
Investment control		
Distribution control		
Estate planning		
Creditor protection		
Medical planning		
Ability to pay for private elementary and secondary school		
Financial aid availability		
Ability to fund for special needs		

The "Yes/No" determinations were made from the parents' perspective, not the student's. "Yes" does not mean "always," but as an advisor you should consider it to mean such. And, as is typically the case, there are exceptions to the rule.

With respect to the "Medical Planning" category, the answer refers to the custodian/owner's ability to take the funds back to use for his own medical needs.

THE COLLEGE FINANCIAL AID HISTORY COMPARISON™

The purpose of the College Financial Aid History Comparison™ (Figure 8.8) is to assist parents who expect to receive need-based financial aid in evaluate colleges during the college selection process. It is important for these families to know which colleges have the money to give. There is, however, some research necessary that can be accomplished through the College Board's website as follows:

1. open the web-browser and go to www.collegeboard.com;

2. type in the name of the college you wish to learn about, and click the "College" button to search their list of colleges;

Figure 8.7
The College Planning Tools/Benefits Grid™

Tool	Tax Benefits		Financial Aid Friendly?	Control		Estate Planning	Elementary/ Secondary School Use	Creditor Protection	Special Needs	Medical Plng
	Gr	Dist		Inv.	Dist.					
529 Plans										
Savings	Y	Y	Y	N	Y	Y	N	Y	Y	Y
Prepaid	Y	Y	Y	N	Y	Y	N	Y	N	Y
Coverdell Education Savings Accounts	Y	Y	Y	Y	N	Y	N	Y	Y	N
UGMA/UTMA	N	N	N	Y	N	Y	Y	Y	Y	N
Life Insurance	Y	Y	Y	Y	Y	Y	Y	Y	Y	Y
Series EE & Series I Savings Bonds	Y	Y	N	Y	Y	N	N	N	N	Y
Roth IRA	Y	N	N	Y	Y	N	N	N	N	Y
Traditional IRA	Y	N	N	Y	Y	N	N	N	N	Y

Dist: Distributee
Gr: Grantor
Inv: Investor

3.   click on the "College Cost and Financial Aid" box on the college page; and

4.   scroll down past the current college cost information to find (a) the percentage of need met, (b) the mix of scholarships/grants to loans, and (c) any other information you may need.

Remember, parents needing financial aid should look for colleges that can meet as close to 100% of their need as possible to avoid the College Financial Aid Gap™, which is the difference between what the financial aid system says a college should give to the family and what the college is actually in the position to give.

The sad fact is that not all colleges are created equal when it comes to financial aid. Some have more money than others, and depending on how many students might qualify for need-based aid, a school may or may not have enough to go around. Federal and state financial aid is limited and if the college does not have a large endowment fund, a family might find that they have to make up the difference.

Figure 8.8

The College Financial Aid History Comparison™					
School Name	Average Financial Aid Package in ($)	% of Need Met	% of Aid in Grants	% of Aid in Loans or Jobs	Forms Required (Circle all that apply)
	$	%	%	%	FAFSA PROFILE College Form
	$	%	%	%	FAFSA PROFILE College Form
	$	%	%	%	FAFSA PROFILE College Form
	$	%	%	%	FAFSA PROFILE College Form
	$	%	%	%	FAFSA PROFILE College Form
	$	%	%	%	FAFSA PROFILE College Form
	$	%	%	%	FAFSA PROFILE College Form
	$	%	%	%	FAFSA PROFILE College Form
	$	%	%	%	FAFSA PROFILE College Form
	$	%	%	%	FAFSA PROFILE College Form
	$	%	%	%	FAFSA PROFILE College Form

THE FINANCIAL AID PLANNING CHECKLIST™

Families likely to qualify for need-based financial aid may have an opportunity to enhance their eligibility if they start planning early enough in the process. The Financial Aid Planning Checklist™ (Figure 8.9) contains suggested areas in which adjustments to a family's financial circumstances might help.

As mentioned earlier in this book, some asset transfer strategies that are designed to improve need-based aid eligibility can be risky and should be approached with extreme caution. Fraud in completing the FAFSA is a punishable offense and may lead to fines and even jail time. At the very least, families who apply to schools that use the Institutional Methodology (IM), or a hybrid of the IM, could reduce the aid coming from those colleges because of additional questions these schools might ask. Families counting on need-based aid above and beyond that provided by federal and state sources may find their financial aid offer lower than expected because it includes assets that the college actually counted when awarding their own endowment money. A family who moves cash assets to an insurance product may suddenly find they cannot access that money to pay their portion of the bill without paying surrender charges and reducing the value of their asset.

For more information about some of these options, refer to Crisis College Plans in Chapter 4. In addition, the Dillon Family case study in Chapter 4 may also contain financial aid planning strategies.

THE COLLEGE CASH FLOW PLANNING CHECKLIST™

The **College Cash Flow Planning Checklist™** (Figure 8.10) is a form designed to assist parents and their advisor find funding resources to pay for college. Once the student has been accepted, the financial aid package accepted, and the deposit has been sent to the school, the parents now know exactly what they will be expected to pay for the upcoming school year.

The checklist is not an exhaustive list. It is simply intended to serve as a guideline. Parent may need the help of a financial professional in evaluating some of the choices. In addition, the resources on this list are not in any order of priority. Selection of any particular resource will be subject to the circumstances and feelings of the parents and student. An example of this checklist can be found in the Dillon Family case study (see Chapter 4).

Figure 8.9

Financial Aid Planning Checklist™
Remember that students must apply for financial aid each year. If the student is a marginal financial aid candidate, families might be able to "create" financial aid eligibility by using some of the strategies below to target certain years, such as those years when there would be two students in college at the same time. This is a suggested list, and should not be considered complete.

Reduce Student Assets:	✓ Use funds in UGMA/UTMA accounts for nonparental student expenses.
	✓ Re-title non-UGMA/UTMA accounts in joint name with a parent's Social Security number.
Control Student Income	✓ Federal Methodology will not include up to the first $3,000 of student income.
	✓ Institutional Methodology will impute $1,550 of student income, whether it is earned or not.
Control Parent Income	✓ Difficult for W-2 earnings, but possible if a parent can control when they receive bonuses, commissions, etc.
	✓ Carefully consider that a nonworking spouse returning to work might reduce financial aid by increasing the parents' total income.
	✓ Liquidation of investments may generate taxable income that can negatively affect the following year's financial aid award.
Reduce Parent Assets	✓ Increase mortgage payments—this will not necessarily affect treatment of home equity as an asset, but can reduce cash assets.
	✓ Use caution when considering repositioning of assets to hide them from financial aid. This is a risky strategy that may not work and may also tie up assets and render them unusable for college in later years.
Divorced/ Separated Parents	✓ Have the lower-income parent become the custodial parent and apply for financial aid.
	✓ May not work for schools using the Institutional Methodology as they will ask for the income and assets of the noncustodial parent and stepparent as well.

Figure 8.10

College Cash Flow Planning Checklist™
✓   This is not necessarily a complete list
Financial Aid Package (from college financial aid office) Pell Grant SEOG Grant Perkins Loan Subsidized Stafford Loan Work/Study College/University scholarship/grant College/University loan
Other Scholarships State scholarships/grants Private scholarships (VFW, etc.) Employer scholarships
Savings Parent's Student's
Current Income Parent's Student's
Tax Savings Hope Scholarship Credit Lifetime Learning Credit Student loan interest deduction
Contributions from Relatives Direct tuition payments Gifts (after financial aid award received)
Student Loans (not part of the financial aid package) Unsubsidized Stafford Loans Signature loans State loans
Parent Loans Mortgage refinance (cash out) Home equity loan Home equity line of credit PLUS loan Private loans
Life Insurance Loans
Retirement Accounts Traditional IRA Roth IRA 401(k)
Use careful consideration before using retirement accounts to pay for college. Taxes may be due, premature distributions may result, or future retirement income may be adversely affected. Consult a financial advising expert.

THE FINANCIAL AID PACKAGE EVALUATOR™

The **Financial Aid Package Evaluator™** (Figure 8.11) is a worksheet that enables a parent to evaluate potential errors in a financial aid package. It is used in conjunction with: (1) an actual financial aid offer received from a college; (2) the actual costs reported from a college; and (3) a financial aid test run from data actually submitted to a college, either through the FAFSA or Profile forms.

THE "REAL" GRANDPARENT CONTRIBUTION™

The **"Real" Grandparent Contribution** ™ (Figure 8.12) is a tool to help advisors explain to grandparents the "real" value of their contributions to a college plan. The "real" value is not just the amount the grandparent deposits into the plan, but also the interest earnings and growth on investments compounded over a period of time. Most grandparents don't realize the true value of the compounded growth, which can be especially significant if the contributions are made earlier (rather than later) in the savings period.

This program is an Excel® spreadsheet with the graphic interface page. The Excel® spreadsheet can be used as a template for advisers to design their own custom illustrations for their clients. The graphics page has been included here to make it easier to motivate clients to take action. Examples of how to use the "Real" Grandparent Contribution can be found in Chapter 2 (Thompson case study) and Chapter 5 (Madsen case study).

Important elements of this tool include:

- The pie chart ("Sources of College Funds"), which lets a grandparent see his initial deposit and the investment growth as a percentage of the projected college bill.

- Two bar graphs that illustrate projected future college costs and projected growth of the grandparent's contribution over time.

- A summary of the "real" grandparent contribution in dollars.

Figure 8.11

The Financial Aid Package Evaluator™ College Name: _____		
1. Actual College Costs (from the college)		
2. Family Expected Contribution (Note: Use updated Financial Aid Test™ results. If college uses PROFILE, use Institutional Methodology; otherwise, use federal methodology. Run using numbers from the actual PROFILE or FAFSA input data.)		
3. % Need Met (from the college financial aid package)		
4. Expected Financial Need $((1 - 2) \times 3)$		
5. Actual Total Financial Aid Package (from the college)		
6. % Grants (from the College Board website)		
7. Expected Grants (4×6)		
8. Actual Grants (from the college financial aid package)		
9. % Loans & Jobs (from the College Board website)		
10. Expected Loans & Jobs (4×9)		
11. Actual Loans & Jobs (from the college financial aid package)		

Figure 8.12

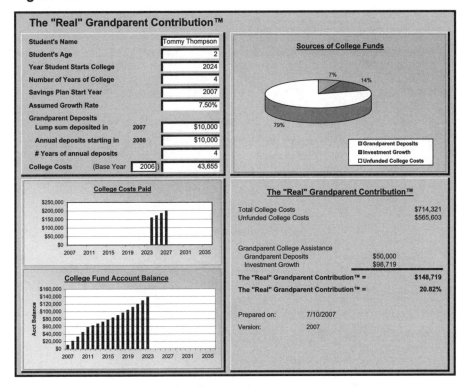

The "Real" Grandparent Contribution™

Student's Name	Tommy Thompson
Student's Age	2
Year Student Starts College	2024
Number of Years of College	4
Savings Plan Start Year	2007
Assumed Growth Rate	7.50%

Grandparent Deposits
Lump sum deposited in 2007 $10,000
Annual deposits starting in 2008 $10,000
Years of annual deposits 4
College Costs (Base Year 2006) 43,655

Sources of College Funds

7%
14%
79%

☑ Grandparent Deposits
☑ Investment Growth
☐ Unfunded College Costs

College Costs Paid

$250,000
$200,000
$150,000
$100,000
$50,000
$0
2007 2011 2015 2019 2023 2027 2031 2035

College Fund Account Balance

$160,000
$140,000
$120,000
$100,000
$80,000
$60,000
$40,000
$20,000
$0
Acct Balance
2007 2011 2015 2019 2023 2027 2031 2035

The "Real" Grandparent Contribution™

Total College Costs	$714,321
Unfunded College Costs	$565,603

Grandparent College Assistance
Grandparent Deposits $50,000
Investment Growth $98,719

The "Real" Grandparent Contribution™ = $148,719
The "Real" Grandparent Contribution™ = 20.82%

Prepared on: 7/10/2007
Version: 2007

Figure 8.12 (Cont'd)

The "Real" Grandparent Contribution™ Calculations

Year	Lump Sum (Start of Yr)	Annual Deposit (Start of Yr)	College Costs Paid (Start of Yr)	Growth (From Prior Yr)	Account Balance (Start of Yr)	Unfunded College
2007	$10,000				$10,000	
2008		$10,000	$0	$750	$20,750	
2009		$10,000	$0	$1,556	$32,306	
2010		$10,000	$0	$2,423	$44,729	
2011		$10,000	$0	$3,355	$58,084	
2012		$0	$0	$4,356	$62,440	
2013		$0	$0	$4,683	$67,123	
2014		$0	$0	$5,034	$72,157	
2015		$0	$0	$5,412	$77,569	
2016		$0	$0	$5,818	$83,387	
2017		$0	$0	$6,254	$89,641	
2018		$0	$0	$6,723	$96,364	
2019		$0	$0	$7,227	$103,591	
2020		$0	$0	$7,769	$111,361	
2021		$0	$0	$8,352	$119,713	
2022		$0	$0	$8,978	$128,691	
2023		$0	$0	$9,652	$138,343	
2024		$0	$158,734	$10,376	$0	$10,015
2025		$0	$171,290	$0	$0	$171,290
2026		$0	$184,839	$0	$0	$184,839
2027		$0	$199,459	$0	$0	$199,459
2028		$0	$0	$0	$0	
2029		$0	$0	$0	$0	
2030		$0	$0	$0	$0	
2031		$0	$0	$0	$0	
2032		$0	$0	$0	$0	
2033		$0	$0	$0	$0	
2034		$0	$0	$0	$0	
2035		$0	$0	$0	$0	
2036		$0	$0	$0	$0	
Totals	$10,000	$40,000	$714,321	$98,719		$565,603

Student Name Tommy Thompson

Date Prepared 7/10/07

Summary Data

Total College Cost7	$714,321
Grandparent Deposits	50,000
Investment Growth	98,719
Unfunded College Costs	$565,603

Appendix A

COLLEGE MONEY COLLEGE COST SURVEY METHODOLOGY

Every year, College Money does a survey of current costs using of a group of representative colleges. Our purpose is to develop a way to help parents and financial advisors build college savings plans that are reality-based rather than simply guesswork.

HOW MUCH DOES COLLEGE *REALLY* COST?

Finding accurate and consistent data for the College Money Annual College Cost Survey is not always easy. We do make every effort to gather data of which we are confident. The following is our typical methodology.

The College Money Benchmark Colleges

We base the survey on 24 purposefully chosen benchmark colleges. First, they are representative of different strata of colleges, many of which are typical colleges that students are likely to attend. Many of the colleges in a range will have similar costs; however, one can often find colleges in one of these categories that vary from the general majority. The six college types that College Money has developed illustrate the typical range of costs. These types are:

1. Community Colleges

2. Low Cost: state colleges for in-state students

3. Medium/Low Cost: state colleges for out-of-state students

4. Medium Cost: small, private colleges

5. Medium/High: larger, private colleges

6. High Cost: Ivy League and Ivy League-type colleges

By using categories, parents and advisors can get a handle on the range of options they actually have when it comes to saving for college. There is no need to save for an Ivy League type school if that isn't the student's aspiration.

Statistically it is also not advisable to base a college savings goal on one specific college. Trends throughout history demonstrate that colleges can manipulate their costs from year to year. Most colleges control three cost centers: (1) tuition, (2) fees, and (3) room and board. Thus, a college can keep down tuition, but raise fees or room and board to compensate for rising costs. In early 2007, Princeton announced that it is freezing tuition for the upcoming year. But the press release did not include the fact that room and board costs increased 4.2%.

By choosing a school for each cost category in four geographic regions of the country, we can smooth out the peaks and valleys of projecting costs. Experience over the past 12 years has shown that college costs tend to be largely uniform across geographic regions. The exception is that state college costs for in-state residents tend to be lower than average in the south, and college costs across all categories on the whole are higher in the northeast. Our survey uses the following geographic regions:

1.   Northeast

2.   Midwest

3.   South

4.   West

WHAT DOES COLLEGE *REALLY* COST?

The data we are searching for is the college's "budget bill." This is a bill that the college compiles each year in order to determine eligibility for need-based financial aid. A student's Expected Family Contribution (EFC) is compared against the budget bill. If the EFC is lower than the budget bill, then the student has demonstrated financial need. On the other hand, if the EFC is higher than the budget bill, then the calculation has indicated that the family can afford to pay the costs to attend that particular college. The costs that are typically included in the budget bill are:

•   Tuition and fees

•   Room and board

•   Books

•   Personal expenses

•   Transportation

Note: Not all colleges include a figure for transportation. In those instances, we use an estimated number based on similar colleges. Even though a college does not report a cost does not mean that the cost doesn't exist. Our intention is to be able to estimate college costs that represent what the majority of students will pay.

Our first step in identifying college costs is to search the individual benchmark colleges' websites for these costs. Issues that can prevent us from obtaining the numbers we need include the following:

- The college website is not updated for the current year.

- The college may have multiple campuses with differing costs for each. Therefore, we choose the main campus wherever possible.

- Different academic programs within a university may have different costs.

- The college may list costs for tuition, fees, and room and board, only.

If we meet any of these obstacles, our next step is to call the school directly. Experience has shown that frequently the only information the employees in the business office can offer is tuition, fees, and room and board.

Our next source is to contact the financial aid office since they are should have access to the "budget bill" each year as explained above. Again, we may be unsuccessful in acquiring the necessary information from this source.

Our final option is to go to public sources that publish this information on a website. We have even experienced missing data with these sources as well. At this point we estimate a number that seems to be comparable to data that similar colleges report.

In considering the price tag of sending a child to college, many parents only consider the tuition or fees they will be responsible for paying. To put a value on the total cost of attendance, all expenses must be taken into account, as the College Money College Cost Survey does. For example, some parents shift some of the costs to the student, such as books, fraternity or sorority dues, and car insurance. Others will foot the bill for everything. Moreover, there are some extraordinary costs that no one even considers, like spring break!

Our experience has also taught us that parents find there are additional costs that are integral to a college education. These include sorority and fraternity dues, costs associated with the cultural experience of the surrounding city, the salary of the local pizza delivery guy, and other social activities. We call this "pizza money." However another way to look at it is as "networking" money. The value of a college education is not simply the academic experience. Many students meet and form friendships with other students who can and will be very instrumental in advancing their career. If a student is unable to participate in social networking, he or she can miss a critical opportunity in their lives. Consequently, we do include a "networking money" factor in our projections; however we do not include spring break. Colleges, on the other hand do not include either cost.

It really does not matter who pays for these additional expenses, they are part and parcel of a student's tenure at college. Some parents just give their student a credit card and pay the bill for them, while others insist that their student earn his or her own spending money. It doesn't matter where the money is coming from; it is all a part of the cost of a college education. As a result, we include a "pizza money" factor in our college cost projections.

PROJECTIONS

The trend in college costs has not changed much over the past 30 years and will not change in the foreseeable future. Costs keep escalating with no end in sight for parents. There have been some periods when the increases have been more startling than others (most recently for example). While college inflation has increased slightly this year, we are not seeing the double-digit hikes across the board. State college costs, however, seem to be ascending more aggressively than those of private colleges

Will college inflation continue to bound upwards, virtually unchecked? Historically, general inflation has been higher than college inflation only four times since 1971. It seems inevitable that this trend will continue in the near future. As the number of students attending four-year colleges increases, colleges have increased operational expenses, which they ultimately pass on to the students. The laws of supply and demand tell us that as long as there are students wanting to go to college, there will be little incentive for colleges to try to be more cost-effective.

Consequently, it is critical that parents and advisors recognize the volatility of college costs and plan accordingly. Sound financial planning relies on solid projections so it is important to have good information to form a foundation. While college costs and savings projections will tend to become more accurate as the student is closer to entering college, it is foolish to put off planning and saving in the early years, because the types of college expenses a parent will be assess can be anticipated.

GLOSSARY

Benefit Evaluation Form™ – This is an adjunct to the Family Scholarship Plan™ graphic. Its function is to allow an advisor to record any client feelings regarding potential benefits of the Family Scholarship Plan™.

Crisis Planning – Starting to plan after high school begins.

College Cash Flow Planning Checklist™ – A form designed to assist parents and their advisor find funding resources to pay for college.

College Financial Aid History Comparison – This is a tool that is used to assist parents who expect to receive need-based financial aid in evaluating colleges during the college selection process.

College Planning Conversation™ – This tool helps advisors to (1) quantify parents' college goals, (2) prompt parents to commit to a preliminary college plan, and (3) motivate parents to accelerate action on their college plans based on how college will impact on their retirement.

Family Benefits Consolidation Summary™ –This is a tool used in grandparent-initiated college savings plans (long-term or crisis) to help grandparents plan for: (1) the differing needs of their grandchildren; (2) crisis planning (when need-based aid is likely and unlikely), and (3) long-term savings (when need-based financial aid is likely and unlikely).

Family Scholarship Plan™ – This is a strategy (not a product) that has three main functions: (1) to focus the college planning client's attention on the benefits that a carefully crafted college plan can produce (instead of focusing on the product); (2) to get the client to recognize that different plan beneficiaries may have different needs and, therefore, require different products or tools in their savings plan; and (3) to communicate the college plan to other family members, such as grandparents, aunts, and uncles, who might be motivated to contribute to the college plan.

Financial Aid Appraisal™ – This tool is used to project potential financial aid into the future. Components include: (1) a bar graph showing the estimated cost of college for each year of expected student enrollment; (2) a summary of anticipated changes to the family's financial circumstances; (3) a bar graph showing estimated financial aid during each year of expected enrollment; and (4) a pie chart showing the impact that estimated potential financial aid can have on the total family college bill.

Financial Aid Package Evaluator™ – This worksheet enables a parent to evaluate potential errors in a financial aid package.

Financial Aid Planning Checklist™ – This list contains suggested areas in which adjustments to a family's financial circumstances might help.

Financial Aid Test™ – This is a diagnostic tool that calculates the Parent Expected Contribution (PEC), the Student Expected Contribution (SEC), and the Family Expected Contribution (FEC) under the Federal Methodology and the Institutional Methodology.

Grandparent-Initiated Long-Term Savings Plan – A four-step process that is essentially similar to a Parent-Initiated Long-Term Savings Plan except for the diagnostic step, which involves more data gathering.

Long-Term College Savings – Starting to plan before high school begins.

Parent Expected Contribution – A quantitative estimate of the parents' ability to contribute to post-secondary educational expenses.

Parent-Initiated Crisis Plan™ – A process to help a family decided whether need-based aid is likely or unlikely so that the family can adjust its planning accordingly.

Parent-Initiated Long-Term Savings Plan™ – A four-step process plan that includes the: (1) diagnostic step; (2) plan design step: (3) implementation step; and (4) monitoring step.

"Real" Grandparent Contribution™ – A tool to help advisors explain to grandparents the "real" value of their contributions to a college plan.

Recovery Period – The end of college to the beginning of retirement.

Saving Period – Today through the start of college.

Spending and Borrowing Period – The start of college through the end of college.

Tool/Benefits Grid™ – This is a table that lists some typical college planning tools and their benefits. This tool is used in conjunction with the Family Scholarship Plan™ and the Benefit Evaluation Form™ to choose the right tools to implement in a college plan.

What's your Super Power?

- ► the power to **identify a need**
- ► the power to **formulate a strategy**
- ► the power to **sincerely benefit clients**
- ► the power to **increase your marketing potential**

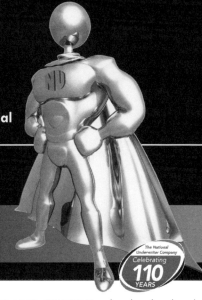

BONUS OFFER!

2 Is Better Than 1

Receive a FREE copy of But What If I Live? The American Retirement Crisis® when you buy HOW TO PLAN for Baby Boomers Power Kit + HOW TO PLAN for College Power Kit Bundle of 2.　(512619K)

The National Underwriter Company
Celebrating **110** YEARS

RETURN POLICY
100% Satisfaction Guaranteed

National Underwriter is confident you'll be pleased with our powerful resources. Your total satisfaction is guaranteed 100% of the time. If your expectations are not met or a product is damaged in shipping, contact us within 30 days from the invoice date for immediate resolution. Your purchase is refundable in the form of your original payment. Special rules apply for certain items:

1) **CE Exams, Electronic Products, CD-ROMs, and Shipping & Handling are not refundable.**

2) **Subscriptions** to newspapers, periodicals and loose-leaf services may be cancelled within 30 days from delivery of a first installment. Loose-Leaf services must be returned for a full refund.

SHIPPING & HANDLING

Order			Total	S&H
$0	to		$39.99	$6.95
$40.00	to		$79.99	$8.95
$80.00	to		$124.99	$11.95
$125.00	to		$199.99	$15.95
$200.00	to		$249.99	$18.95

Add shipping and handling charges to all orders as indicated. If your order exceeds total amount listed in chart, or for overseas rates, call 1-800-543-0874. **Any order of 10 or more items or $250 and over will be billed for shipping by actual weight, plus a handling fee.** Any discounts do not apply to Shipping & Handling.

QTY	ITEM DESCRIPTION	PRODUCT #	RETAIL 1-9	SALE PRICE 10 OR MORE	TOTAL PRICE
	But What If I Live? Book	1890000	$19.95	$17.00	
	HOW TO PLAN for Baby Boomers Book	5120002	$34.95	$31.46	
	HOW TO PLAN for College Book	6190000	$34.95	$31.46	
	Garrett's Guide to Financial Planning Book & CD	2750002K	$47.95	$43.16	
	HOW TO PLAN for Baby Boomers Power Kit	5120002K	$74.95	$67.46	
	HOW TO PLAN for College Power Kit	6190000K	$74.95	$67.46	
	Ultimate IRA Resource Book & CD	2210003K	$74.95	$67.46	
	HOW TO PLAN Power Bundle **(Bonus Offer!)**	512619K	$149.90	$134.91	

Sales Tax: Residents of CA, CT, DC, FL, GA, IL, KS, KY, MI, NJ, NY, OH, PA, TX and WA must add appropriate sales tax

SUBTOTAL $

Shipping & Handling (see chart) $

ORDER TOTAL $

Promo Code: GCARD
Offer Ends 12/30/08.

HOW TO PLAN Power Bundle
Offer Ends 12/30/07.

Discounts are based on a minimum purchase of the same title/product number. If you do not meet the minimum quantity to qualify for the printed discount, you will be invoiced the retail price.

❑ Invoice Me　❑ Call Me

Title _____
E-mail _____
Fax ( ) _____

Company _____
Name _____
Phone ( ) _____
Address _____
City _____ State _____ Zip _____

TOOLS & TECHNIQUES

Brought to you by the publisher of Tax Facts

ROAD TO SUCCESS

Begins with Tools & Techniques

The Disciplined Approach for Today's Professional.

Discover more at www.NUCOstore.com/TandT